FIRST 50 MOVIE SONGS
YOU SHOULD PLAY ON THE PIANO

ISBN 978-1-4950-3588-3

HAL•LEONARD®
CORPORATION
7777 W. BLUEMOUND RD. P.O. BOX 13819 MILWAUKEE, WI 53213

Visit Hal Leonard Online at
www.halleonard.com

CONTENTS

AGAINST ALL ODDS

(Take a Look at Me Now)
from AGAINST ALL ODDS

Words and Music by
PHIL COLLINS

Slow Rock

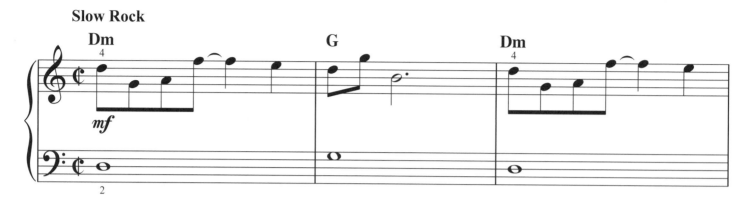

1. How can I just let ___ you walk a - way, just let you
2.,3. *(See additional lyrics)*

leave with - out ___ a trace? When I stand here tak - ing

ev - 'ry breath with you; ___ ooh, ___ you're the

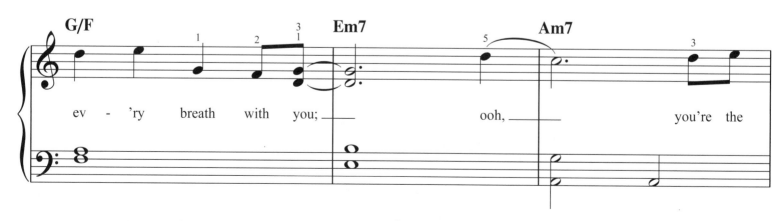

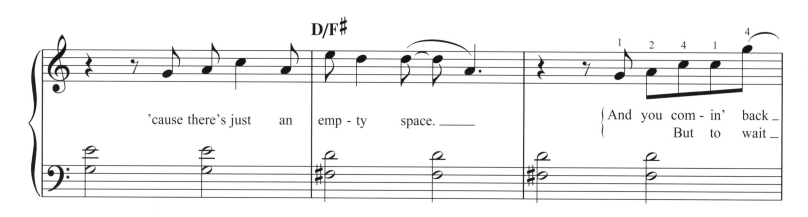

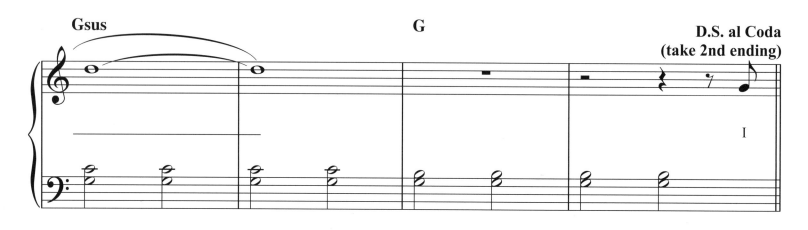

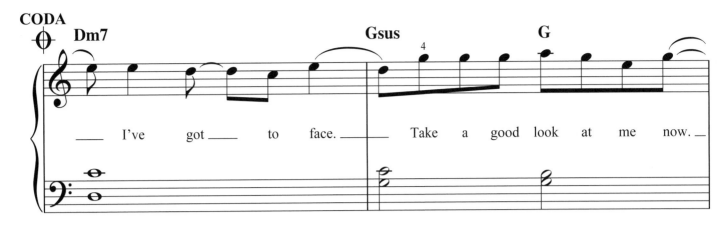

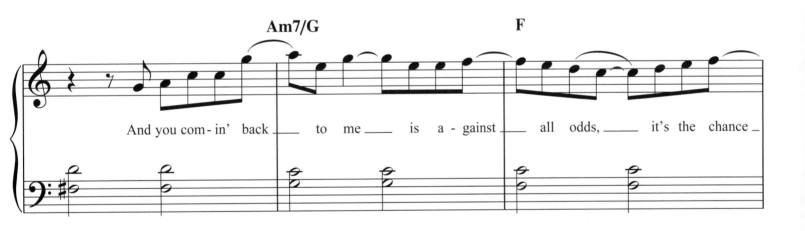

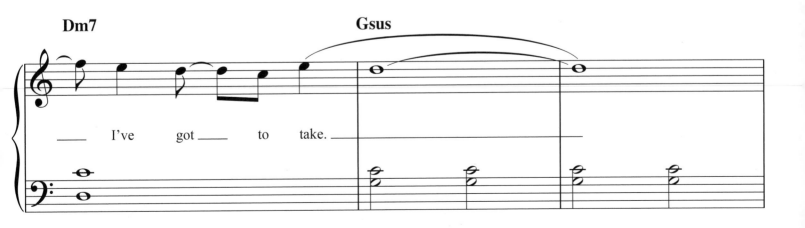

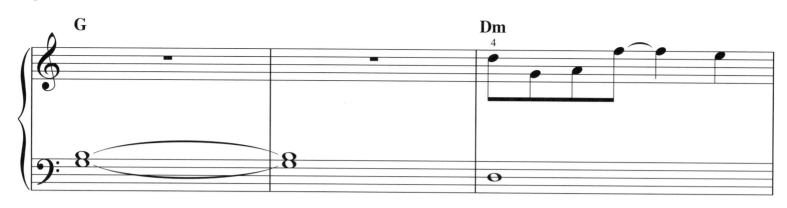

Take a look at me now. _

Additional Lyrics

2. How can you just walk away from me,
   When all I can do is watch you leave?
   'Cause we shared the laughter and the pain,
   We even shared the tears.
   You're the only one who really knew me at all.
   Chorus

3. I wish I could just make you turn around,
   Turn around and see me cryin',
   There's so much I need to say to you,
   So many reasons why.
   You're the only one who really knew me at all.
   Chorus

AS TIME GOES BY

from CASABLANCA

Words and Music by
HERMAN HUPFELD

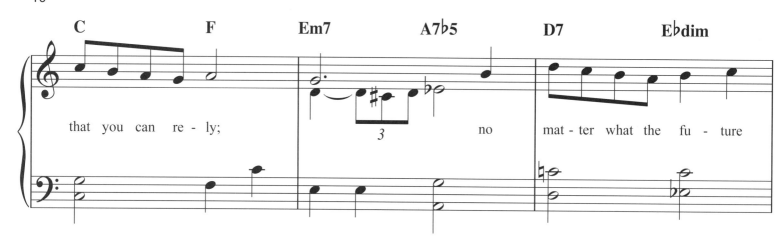

that you can re - ly; no mat - ter what the fu - ture

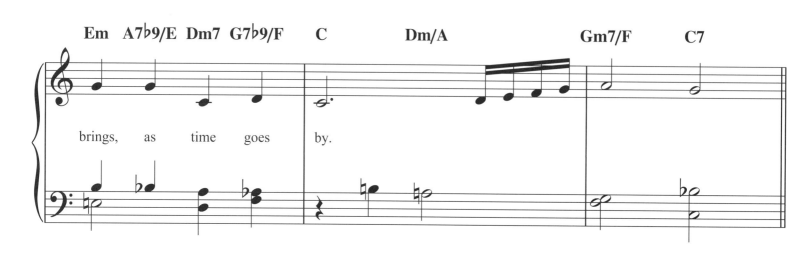

brings, as time goes by.

Moon-light and love __ songs nev - er out of date, hearts full of pas - sion,

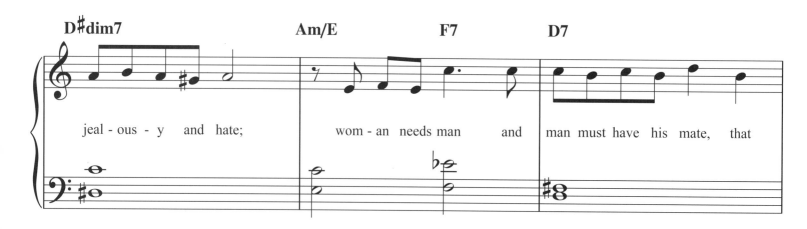

jeal - ous - y and hate; wom - an needs man and man must have his mate, that

11

no one can de - ny.
It's still the same old sto - ry, a

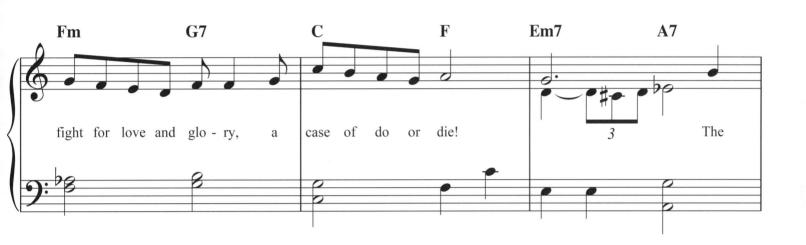

fight for love and glo - ry, a case of do or die! The

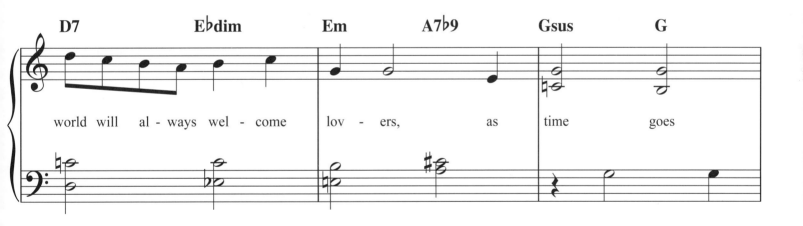

world will al - ways wel - come lov - ers, as time goes

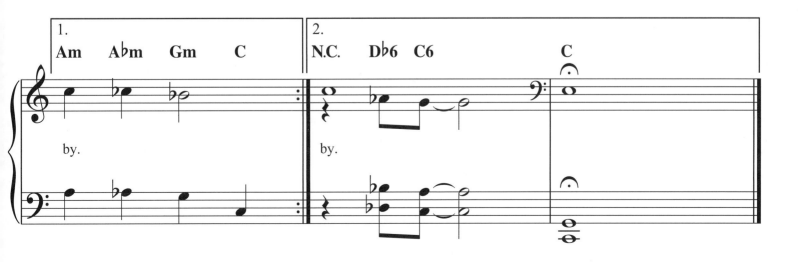

by. by.

ALFIE
Theme from the Paramount Picture ALFIE

Words by HAL DAVID
Music by BURT BACHARACH

Very slowly, Rubato

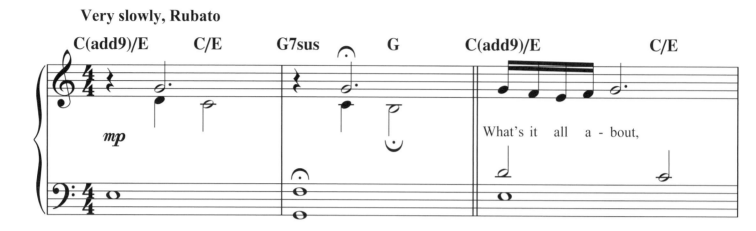

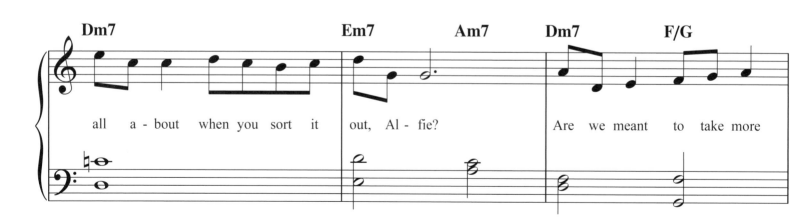

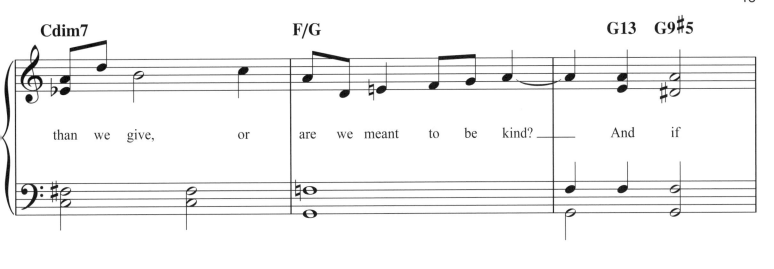

than we give, or are we meant to be kind? ____ And if

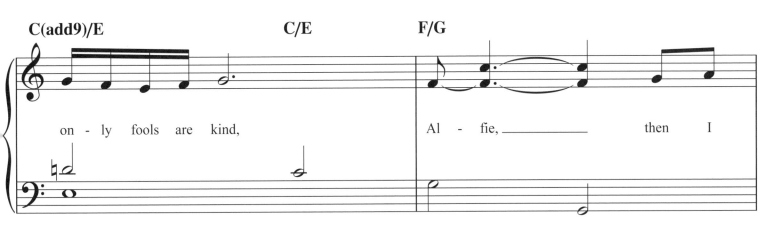

on - ly fools are kind, Al - fie, _____ then I

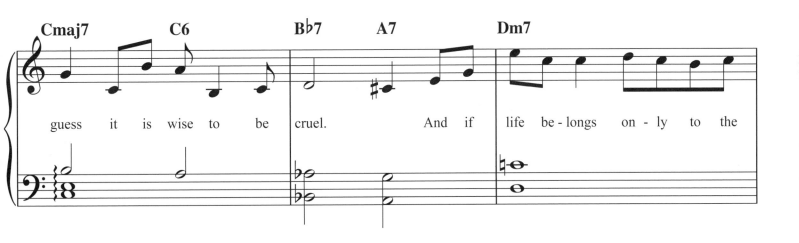

guess it is wise to be cruel. And if life be - longs on - ly to the

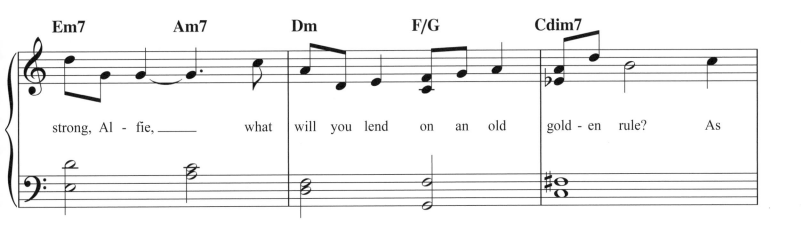

strong, Al - fie, _____ what will you lend on an old gold - en rule? As

sure as I be - lieve there's a heav-en a - bove, Al - fie,

I know there's some-thing much more, some-thing e - ven

non - be - liev - ers can be - lieve in. I be-lieve in love,

Al - fie. _____ With - out true love we just ex -

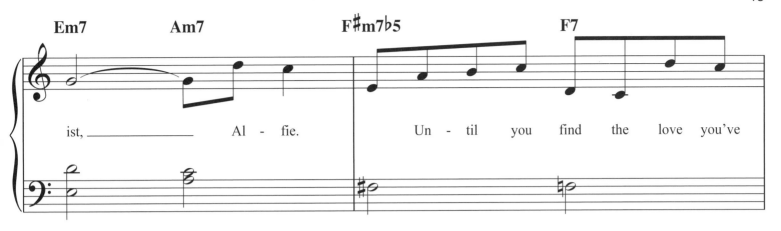

ist, _____ Al - fie.   Un - til you find the love you've

missed you're noth - ing, Al - fie.   When you walk let your heart

rall.   *a tempo*

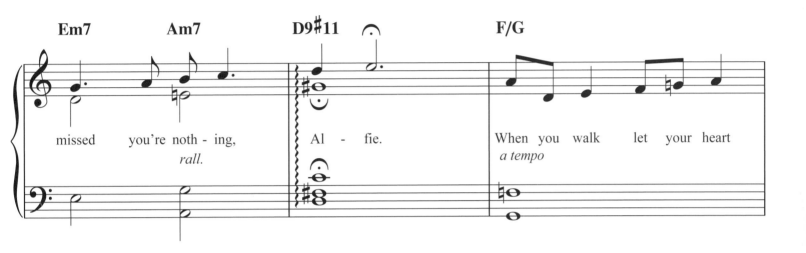

lead the way, and   you'll find love an - y day, Al - fie,

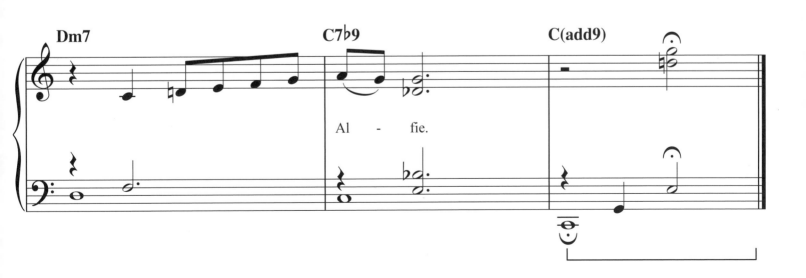

Al - fie.

BECAUSE YOU LOVED ME

from UP CLOSE AND PERSONAL

Words and Music by
DIANE WARREN

For all those times you stood by me, for all the

truth that you made me see, for all the joy you brought to my life, for all the
hand, I could touch the sky. I lost my faith, you gave it back to me. You said no

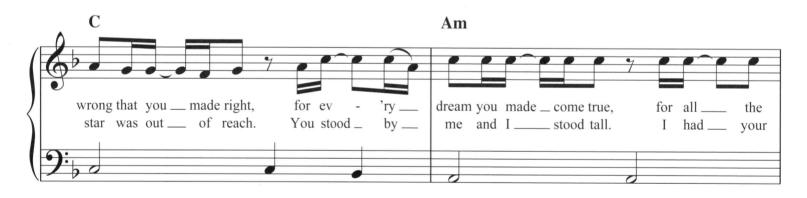

wrong that you made right, for ev - 'ry dream you made come true, for all the
star was out of reach. You stood by me and I stood tall. I had your

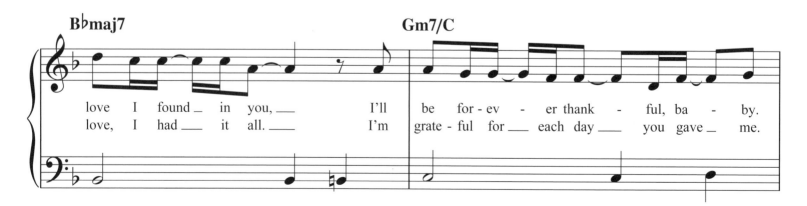

love I found in you, I'll be for - ev - er thank - ful, ba - by.
love, I had it all. I'm grate - ful for each day you gave me.

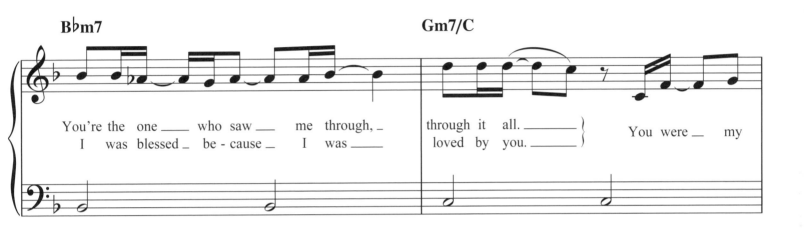

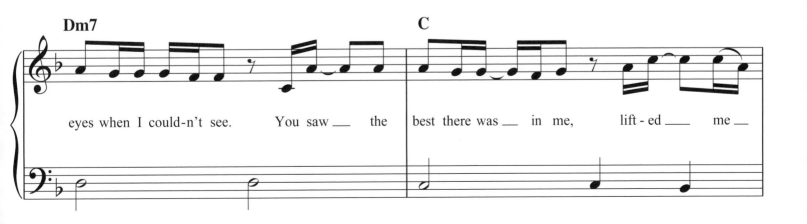

Am   B♭   E♭maj7

up when I could-n't reach.   You gave ___ me   faith 'cause you ___ be - lieved. ___   I'm

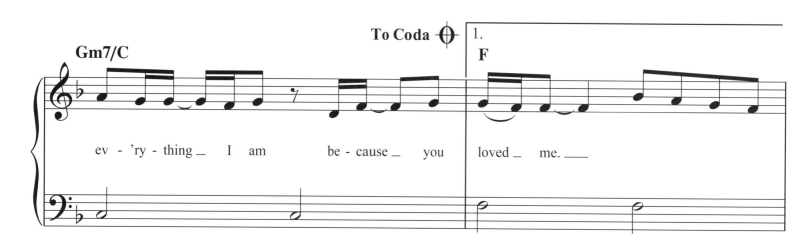

Gm7/C   To Coda ⊕ | 1.
                                                        | F

ev - 'ry - thing ___ I am   be - cause ___ you   loved ___ me. ___

Gm/C | 2.
                                             | F

You gave ___ me   loved ___ me. ___

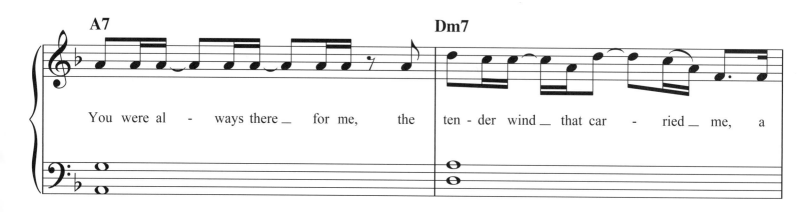

A7   Dm7

You were al - ways there ___ for me,   the   ten - der wind ___ that car - ried ___ me,   a

light in the dark, __ shin-ing your love __ in - to my __ life. _____ You've

been my in - spi - ra - tion. _____ Through the lies, __ you were __ the truth. My

world is a bet - ter place be - cause __ of you. ___ You were __ my

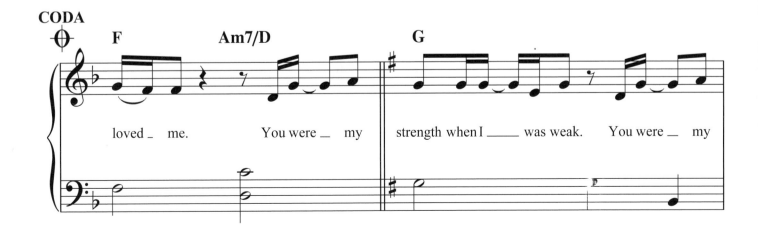

loved __ me. You were __ my strength when I __ was weak. You were __ my

20

voice when I could-n't speak. You were ___ my eyes when I could-n't see. You saw ___ the

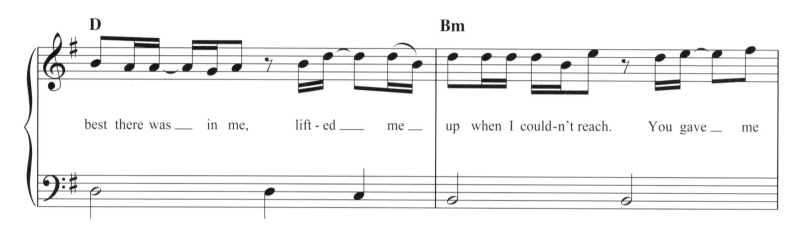

best there was ___ in me, lift-ed ___ me ___ up when I could-n't reach. You gave ___ me

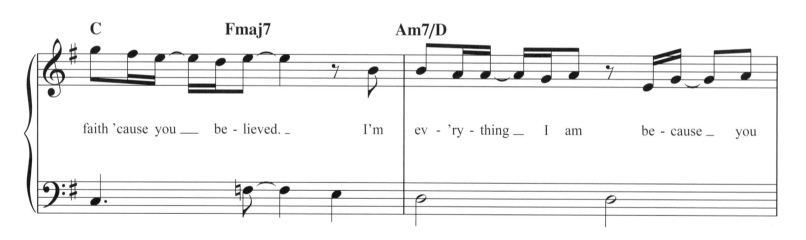

faith 'cause you ___ be-lieved. ___ I'm ev-'ry-thing ___ I am be-cause ___ you

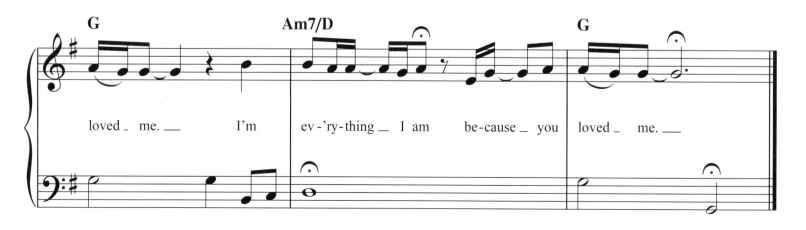

loved _ me. ___ I'm ev-'ry-thing ___ I am be-cause ___ you loved _ me. ___

CRAZY FOR YOU
VISION QUEST

Words and Music by JOHN BETTIS
and JON LIND

Sway - in' room as the
Try - in' hard to con -

mu - sic starts. _
trol my heart, _

Stran - gers mak - in' the most _
I walk o - ver to where _

of the dark. _
you are. _

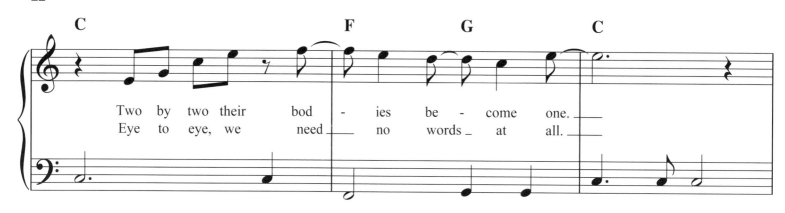

Two by two their bod - ies be - come one.
Eye to eye, we need no words at all.

I see you through the smok - y air.
Slow - ly now we be - gin to move.

Can't you feel the weight of my stare?
Ev - 'ry breath I'm deep - er in - to you.

You're so close but still
Soon we two are stand -

a world a - way.
- in' still in time.

What I'm dy - in' to say is that I'm
If you read my mind, you'll see I'm

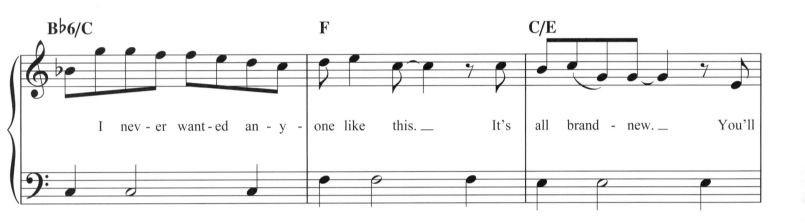

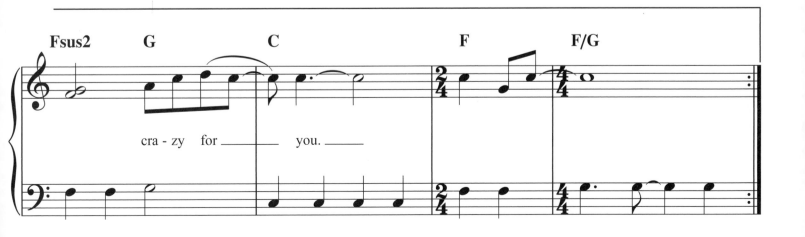

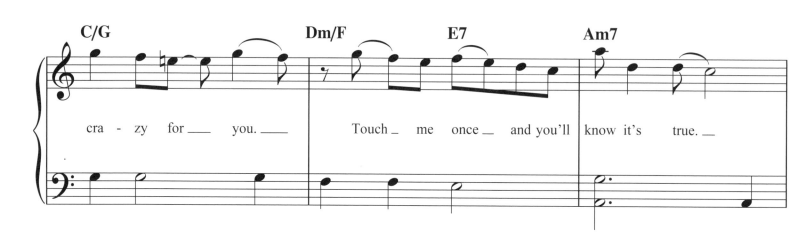

cra - zy for _____ you, _____ cra - zy for you. _

It's all brand - new. _ I'm cra - zy for you. _ And you know it's true. _

_ I'm cra - zy, cra - zy for you. _

BLAZE OF GLORY

featured in the film YOUNG GUNS II

Words and Music by
JON BON JOVI

With a steady Rock beat

morn - ing and I raise my wea - ry head, I've got an

world they say you're born in sin. Well, at

con - science and I of - fer you my soul. You ask if I'll

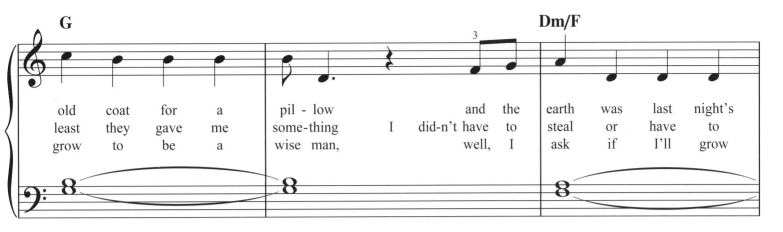

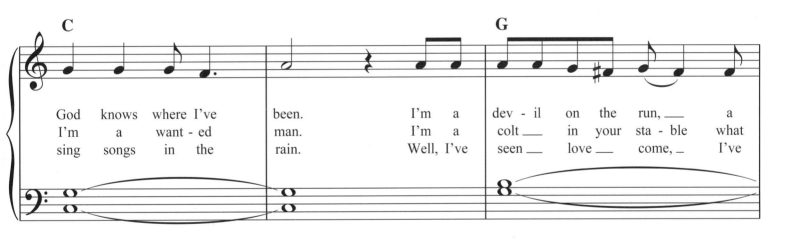

28

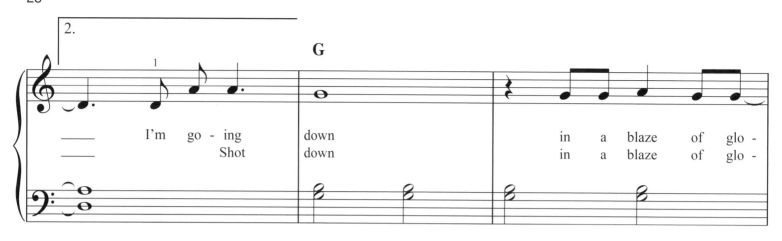

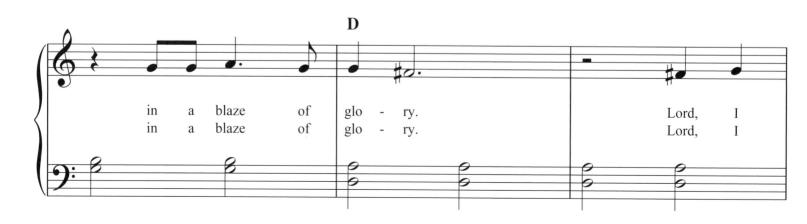

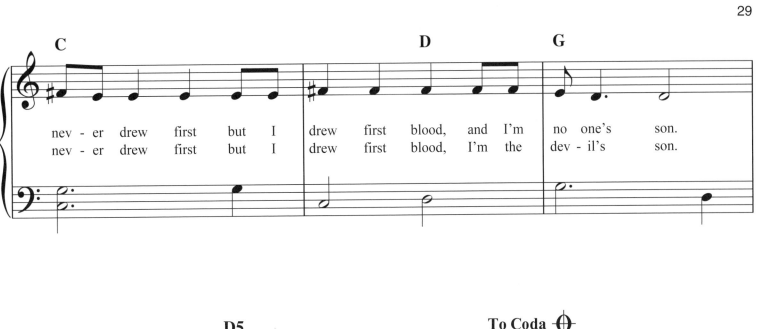

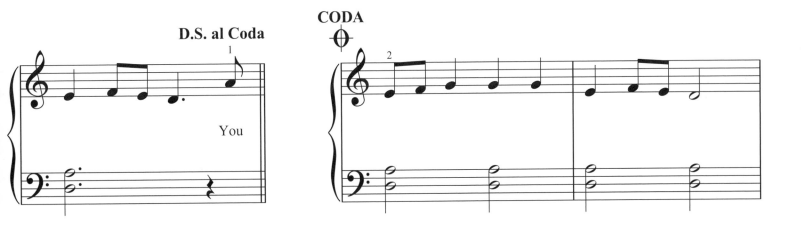

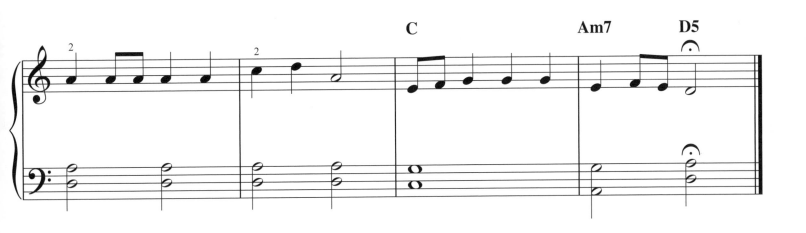

CALL ME
from the Paramount Motion Picture AMERICAN GIGOLO

Words by DEBORAH HARRY
Music by GIORGIO MORODER

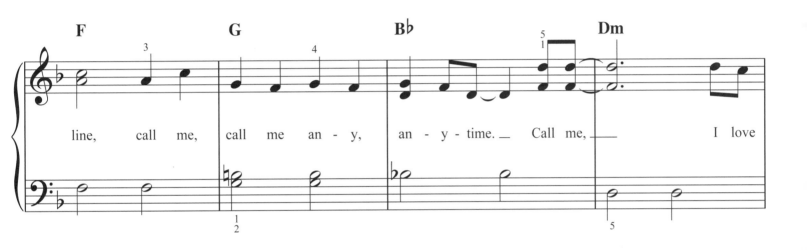

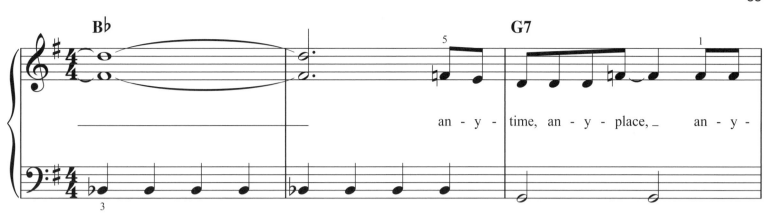

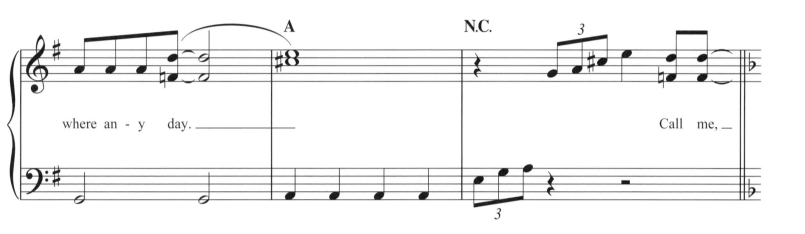

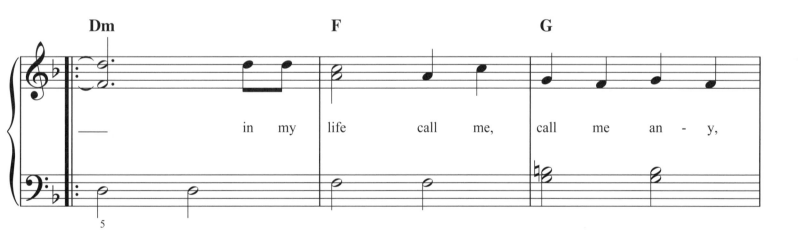

DANGER ZONE
from the Motion Picture TOP GUN

Words and Music by GIORGIO MORODER
and TOM WHITLOCK

Bright Rock

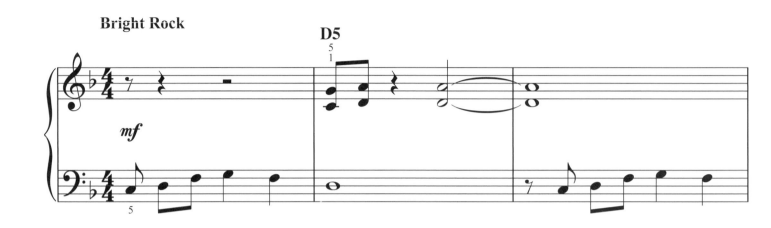

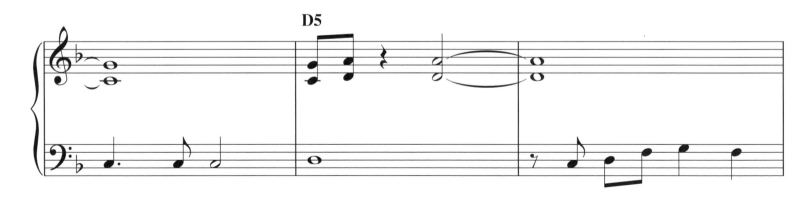

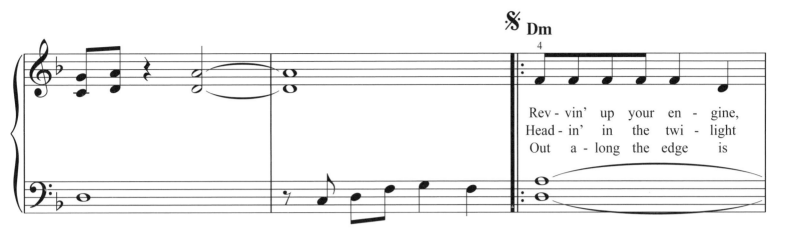

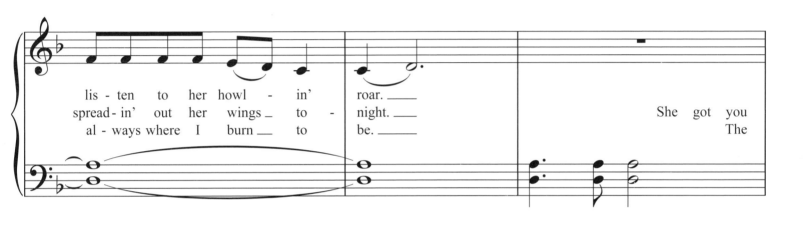

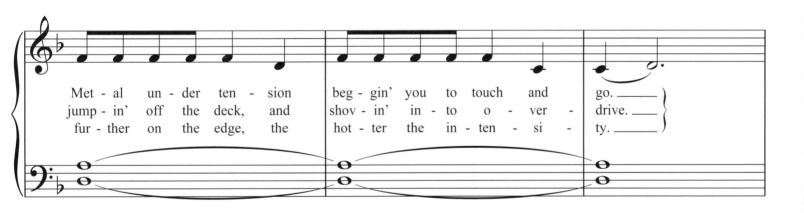

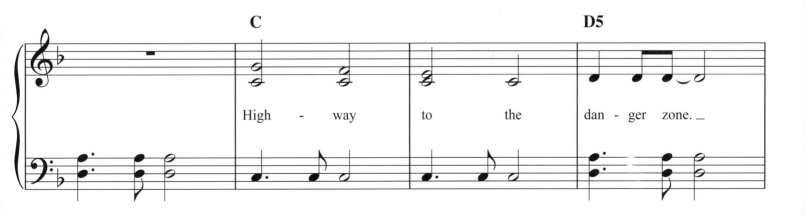

C

To Coda ⊕

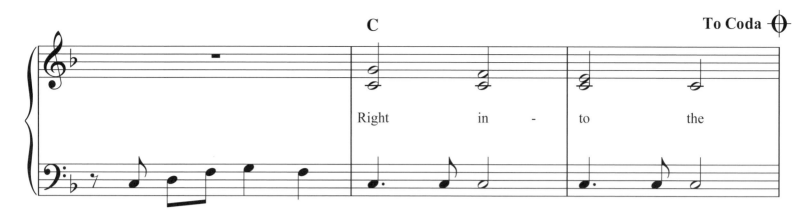

Right in - to the

1.
B♭

dan - ger zone. _____

2.
B♭

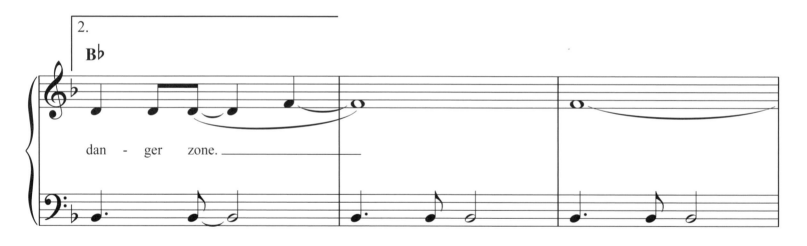

dan - ger zone. _____

G5

You'll nev - er say hel - lo to you ___ un - til you get it on the

red line o - ver - load. You'll nev - er know what you can do

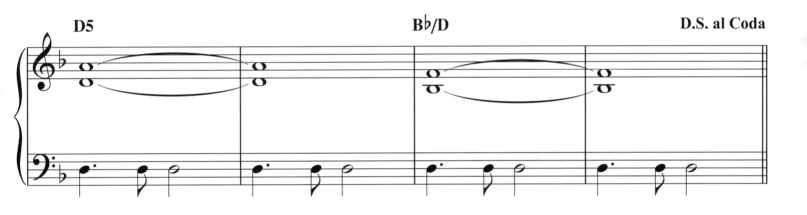

un - til you get it up as high as you can go.

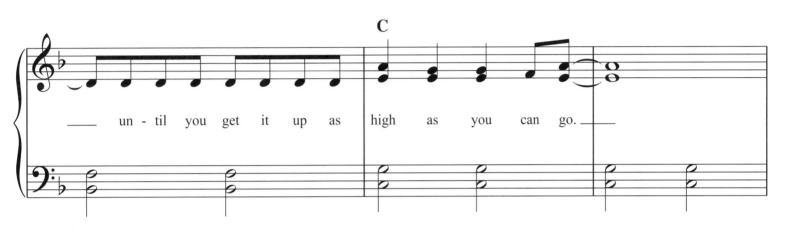

D.S. al Coda

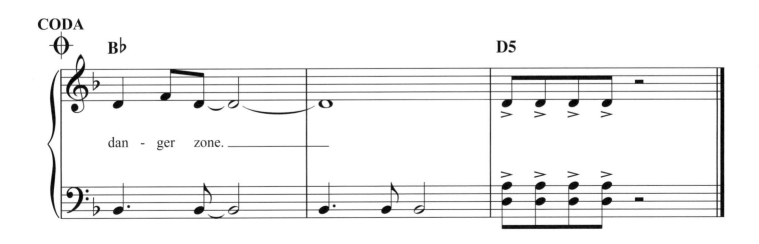

CODA

dan - ger zone.

DON'T YOU
(Forget About Me)
from the Universal Picture THE BREAKFAST CLUB

Words and Music by KEITH FORSEY
and STEVE SCHIFF

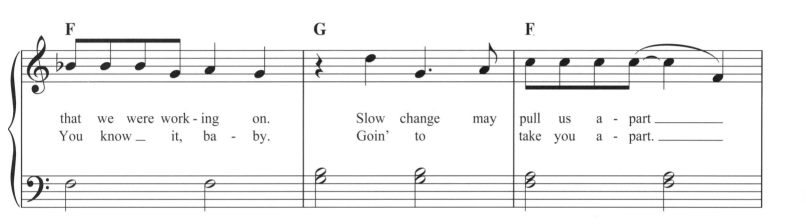

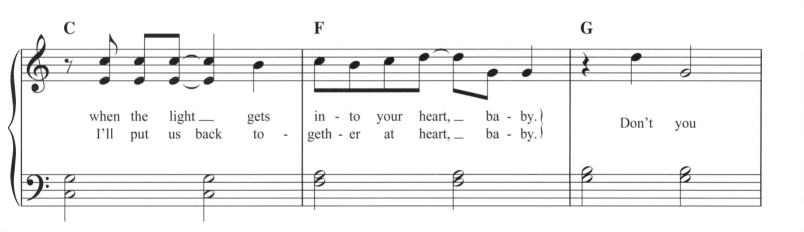

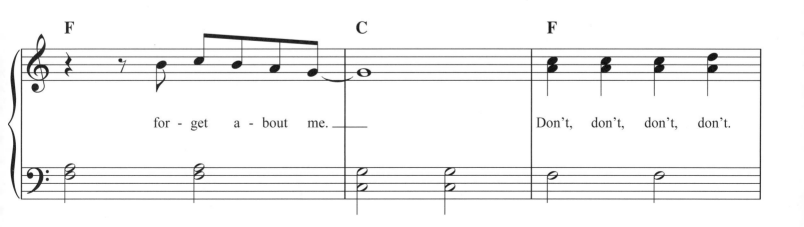

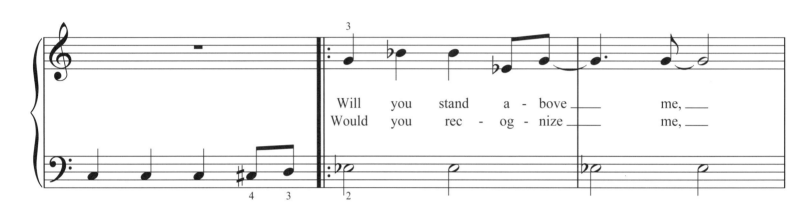

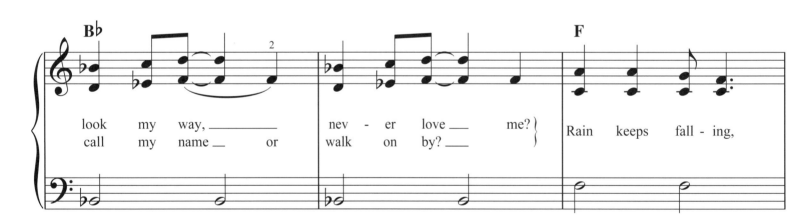

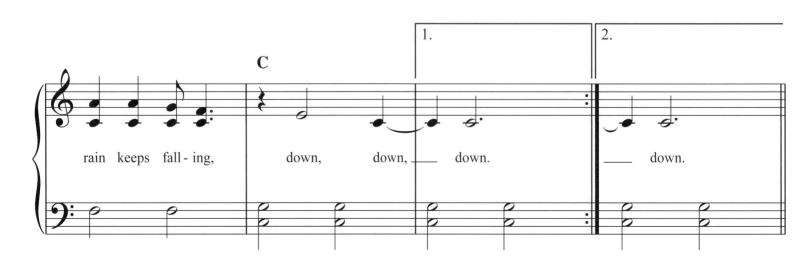

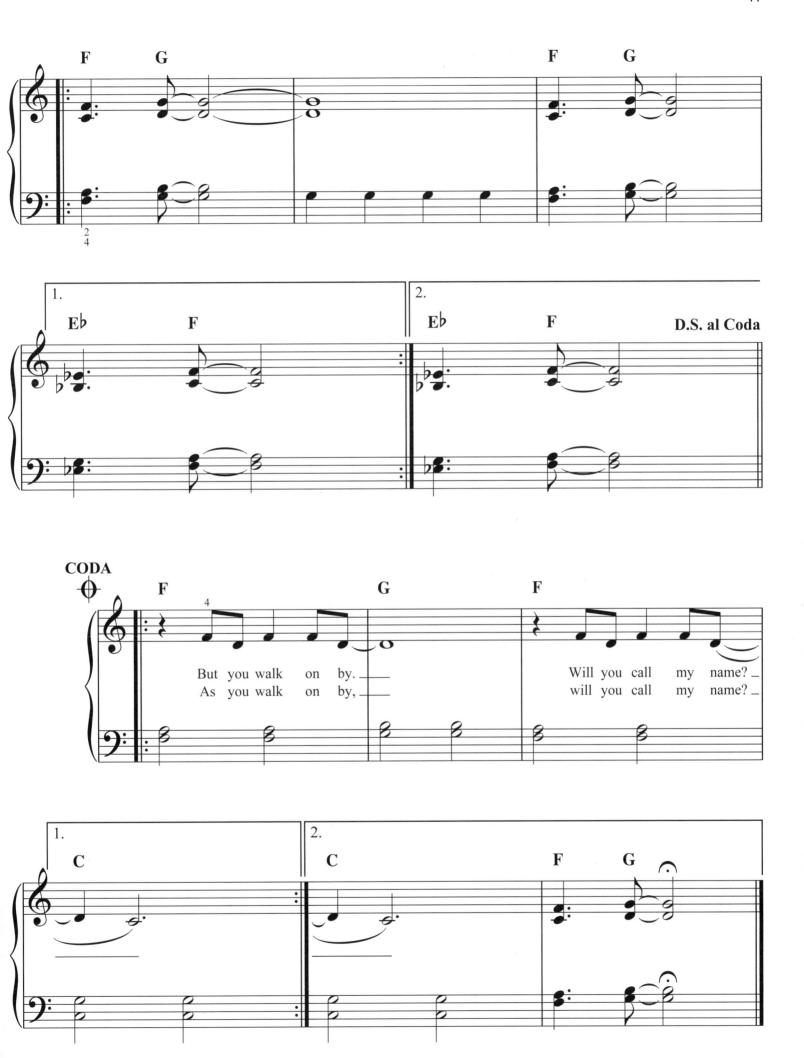

END OF THE ROAD

from the Paramount Motion Picture BOOMERANG

Words and Music by BABYFACE,
L.A. REID and DARYL SIMMONS

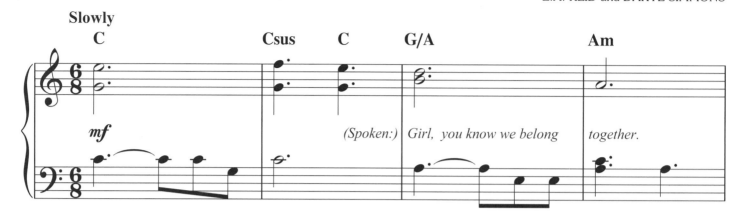

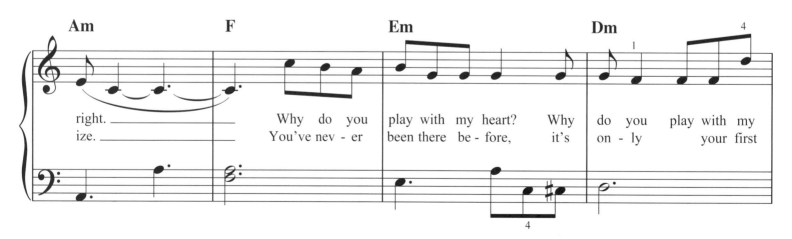

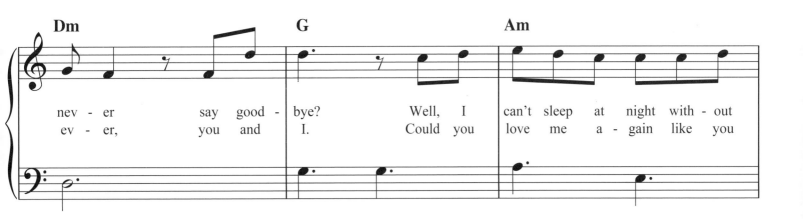

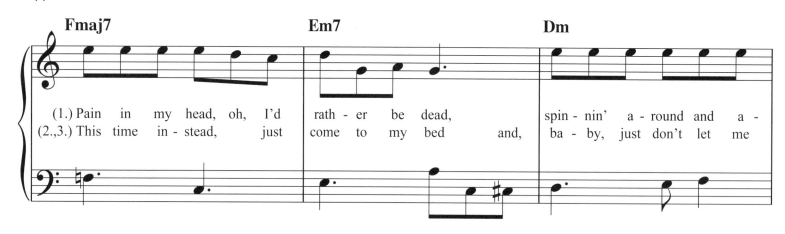

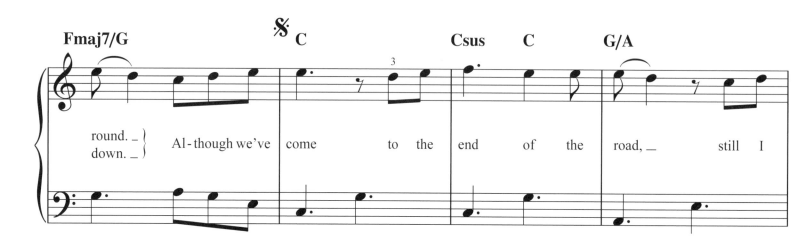

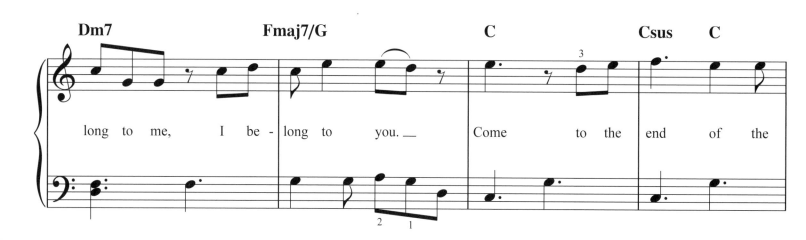

Additional Lyrics

(Spoken:) Girl, I'm here for you.
All those times at night when you just hurt me,
And just ran out with that other fellow,
Baby, I knew about it.
I just didn't care.
You just don't understand how much I love you, do you?
I'm here for you.
I'm not out to go out there and cheat all night just like you did, baby.
But that's alright, huh, I love you anyway.
And I'm still gonna be here for you 'til my dyin' day, baby.
Right now, I'm just in so much pain, baby.
'Cause you just won't come back to me, will you?
Just come back to me.

Yes, baby, my heart is lonely.
My heart hurts, baby yes, I feel pain too.
Baby please...

EYE OF THE TIGER
Theme from ROCKY III

Words and Music by FRANK SULLIVAN
and JIM PETERIK

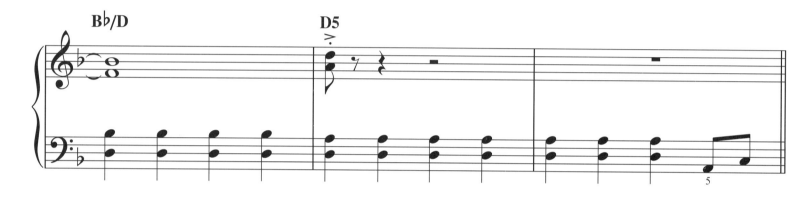

1. Ris - in' up   back on the   street, _____   did my time, took my
2. So man - y times   it   hap - pens too   fast. _____   You trade your pas - sion for
3.-4. *(See additional lyrics)*

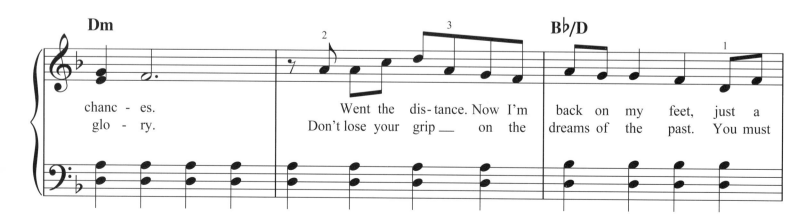

chanc - es.   back on my   feet,   just a
glo - ry.   Went the   dis - tance. Now I'm   back on my   feet,   just a
           Don't lose your grip __ on the   dreams of the   past. You must

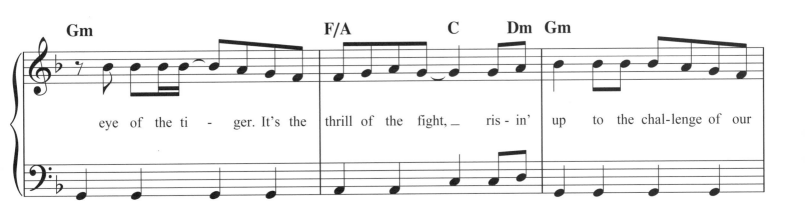

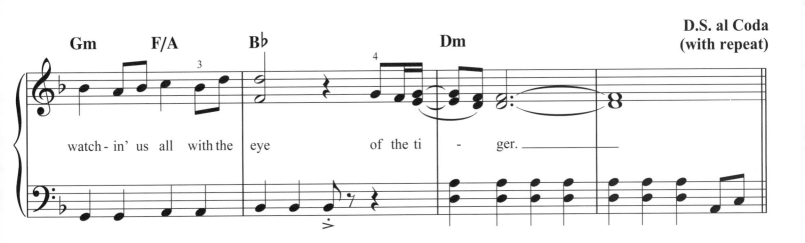

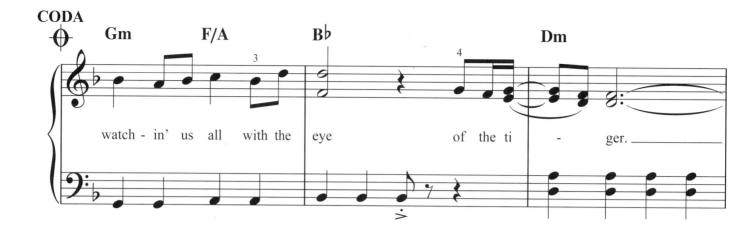

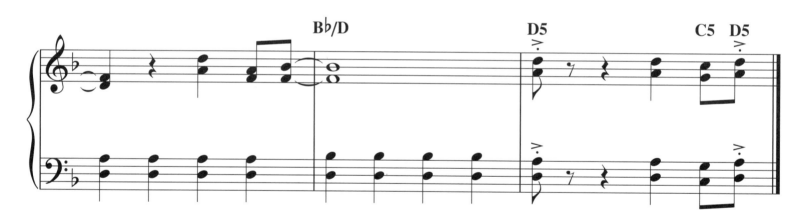

Additional Lyrics

3. Face to face, out in the heat,
   Hangin' tough, stayin' hungry.
   They stack the odds, still we take to the street
   For the kill with the skill to survive.

4. Risin' up, straight to the top.
   Had the guts, got the glory.
   Went the distance. Now I'm not gonna stop,
   Just a man and his will to survive.

ENDLESS LOVE

from ENDLESS LOVE

Words and Music by
LIONEL RICHIE

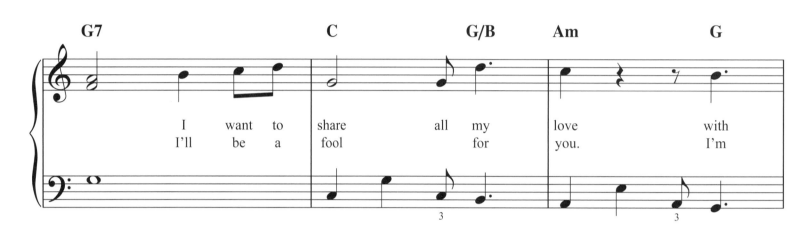

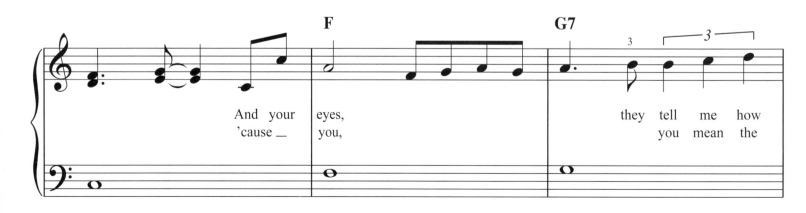

much   you   care.   Oh _____   yes,   you will

world   to   me.   Oh, ___ I   know   I _____

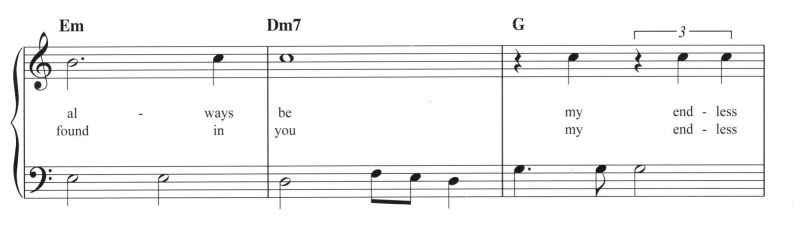

al - ways   be   my   end - less

found   in   you   my   end - less

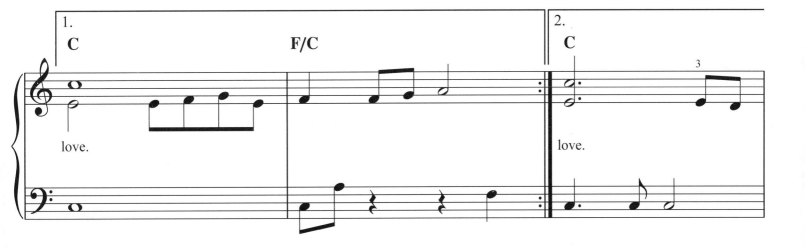

love.   love.

rit.

(Everything I Do)
I DO IT FOR YOU
from the Motion Picture ROBIN HOOD: PRINCE OF THIEVES

Words and Music by BRYAN ADAMS,
R.J. LANGE and MICHAEL KAMEN

Look in - to my eyes, ____ you will see ____
Look in - to my heart, ____ you will find ____ there's

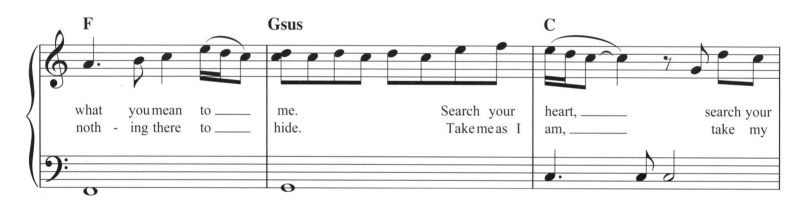

what you mean to ____ me. Search your
noth - ing there to ____ hide. Take me as I

heart, ____ search your
am, ____ take my

soul, ____ and when you find me there you'll ____ search ____ no more. Don't
life, ____ I would give it all, I would sac - ri - fice. Don't

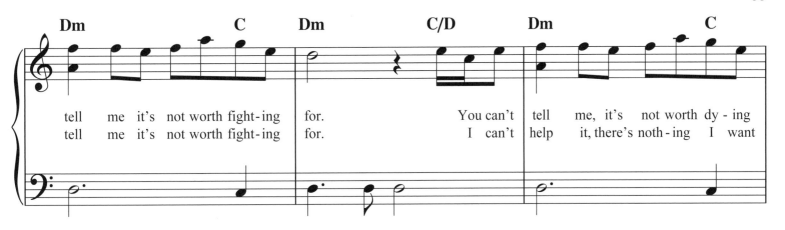

tell me it's not worth fight-ing for. You can't tell me, it's not worth dy-ing
tell me it's not worth fight-ing for. I can't help it, there's noth-ing I want

for. } You know it's true, _____ ev-'ry-thing I do, I do it
more. }

1.
for you. _____

2.
for you. _____ There's

no love like your love, _____ and no oth - er could give

more ___ love. There's no ___ way, ___ un - less you're ___ there all the

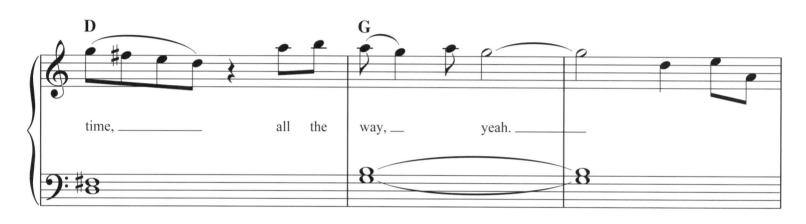

time, _____ all the way, ___ yeah. ___

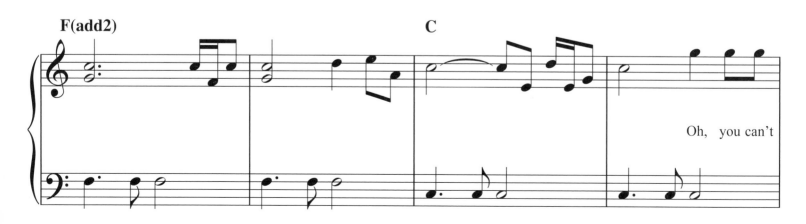

Oh, you can't

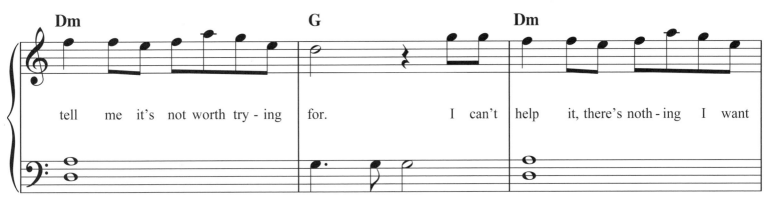

tell me it's not worth try - ing for. I can't help it, there's noth - ing I want

more. Yeah, I would fight __ for you, __ I'd lie _____ for you, __ walk the

wire for you, yeah, I'd die for you. __ You know it's true, ev -'ry-thing I

do, oh, _____ oh, I do it for ___ you.

FLASHDANCE...WHAT A FEELING

from the Paramount Picture FLASHDANCE

Lyrics by KEITH FORSEY and IRENE CARA
Music by GIORGIO MORODER

57

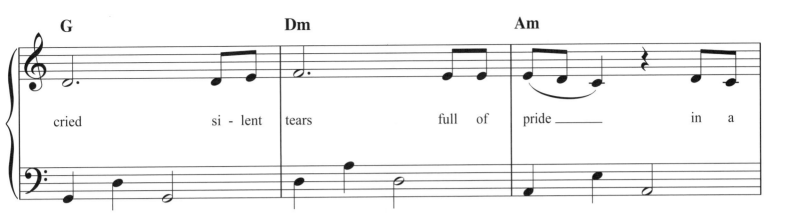

cried   si - lent tears   full of   pride _____   in a

Faster, with a driving beat

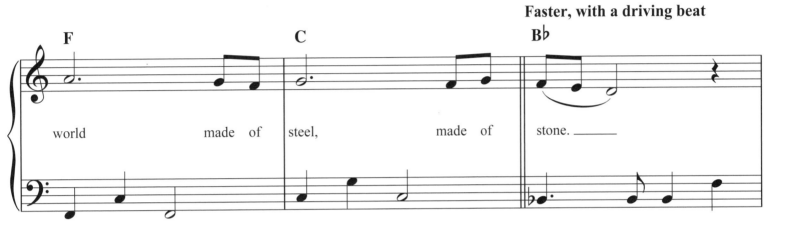

world   made of   steel,   made of   stone. _____

Well, _

I   hear the mu - sic,   close my eyes,   feel the

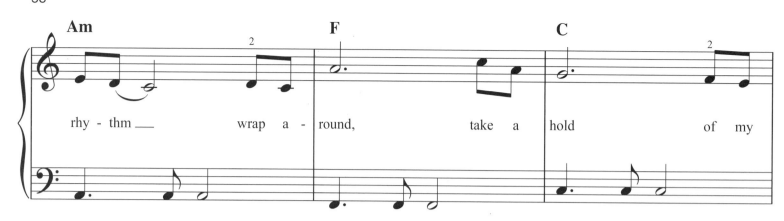

rhy - thm _____ wrap a - round, take a hold of my

heart. _____ What a feel - ing.

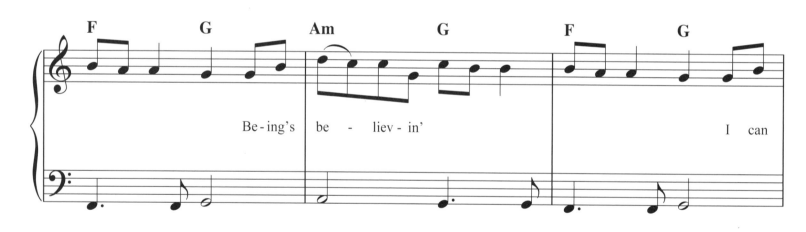

Be - ing's be - liev - in' I can

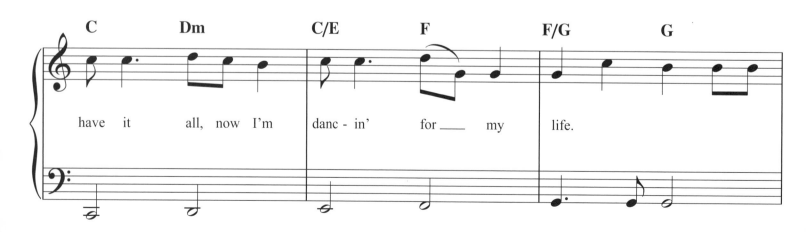

have it all, now I'm danc - in' for _____ my life.

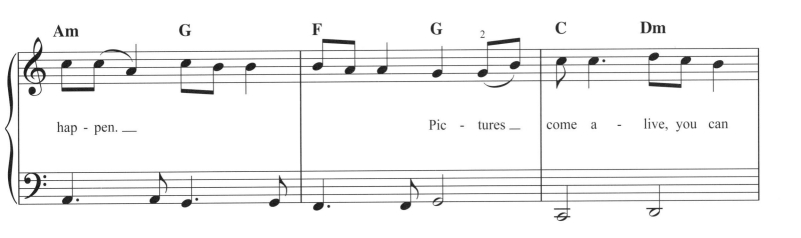

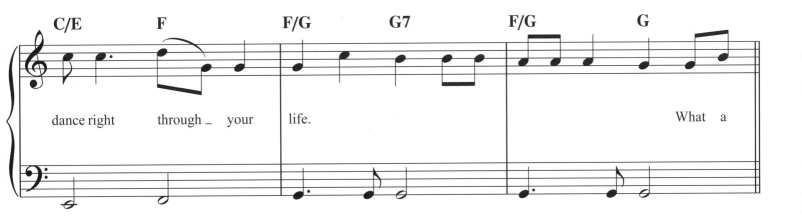

FOOTLOOSE
Theme from the Paramount Motion Picture FOOTLOOSE

Words by DEAN PITCHFORD
Music by KENNY LOGGINS

I been work - in'   so hard.
You're play - in'   so cool,

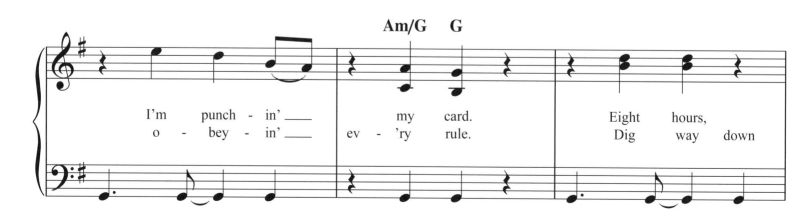

I'm punch - in' ___   my card.
o - bey - in' ___   ev - 'ry rule.

Eight hours,
Dig way down

in   your   heart. / for   what?
You're   burn - in',   Oh,   tell   me / yearn - in'   for   some, / what   I   got.

C

I've   got   this / some - bod - y   to / feel - in' ____   tell   you ____ / that   time's   just / that   life   ain't

G   **C/G**   **G**

hold - in'   me   down. ____ / pass - in'   you   by. ____

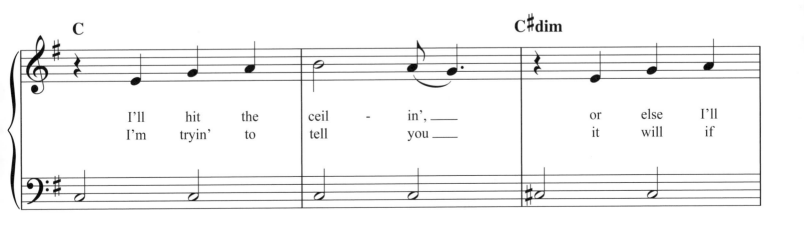

C   **C#dim**

I'll   hit   the / I'm   tryin'   to / ceil - in', ____   tell   you ____ / or   else   I'll / it   will   if

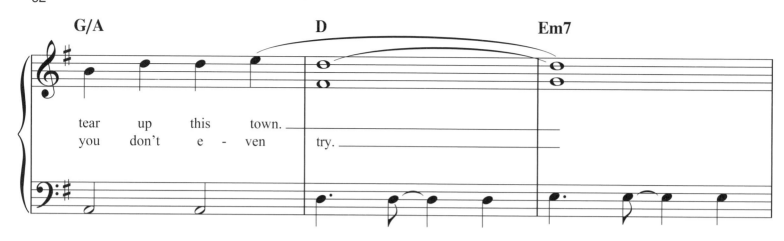

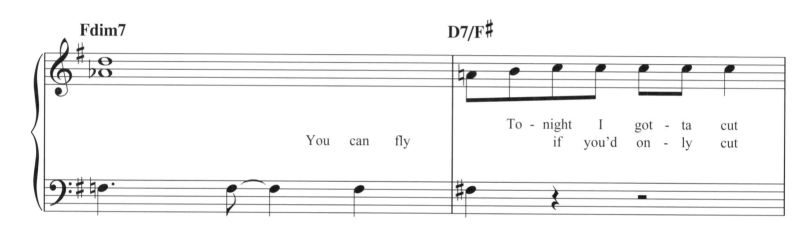

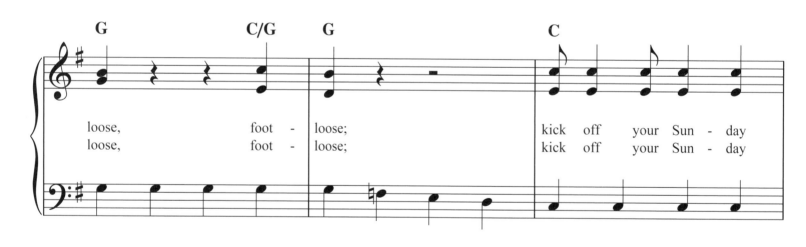

HALLELUJAH
featured in the DreamWorks Motion Picture SHREK

Words and Music by
LEONARD COHEN

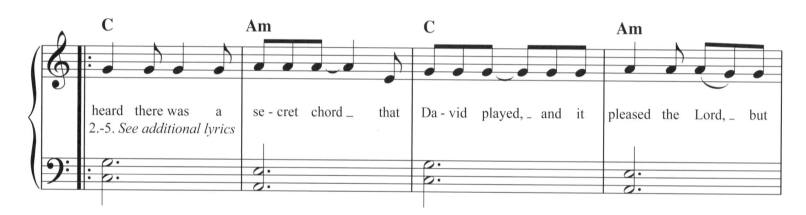

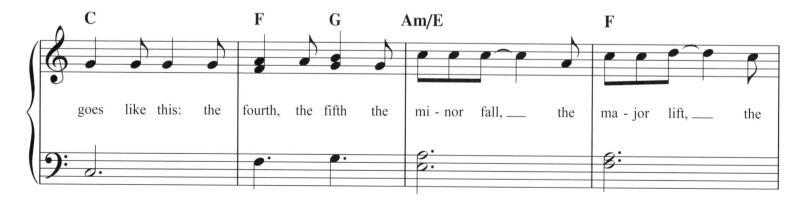

65

CODA

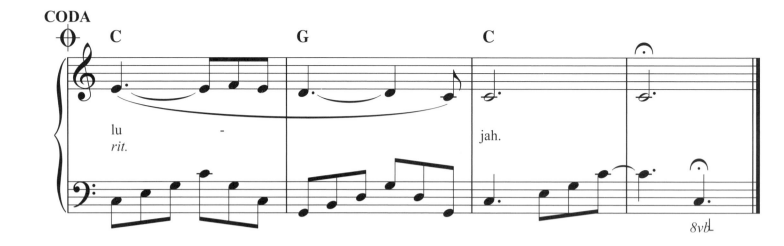

lu -
rit.

jah.

Additional Lyrics

2. Your faith was strong, but you needed proof.
   You saw her bathing on the roof.
   Her beauty and the moonlight overthrew you.
   She tied you to a kitchen chair.
   She broke your throne; she cut your hair.
   And from your lips she drew the Hallelujah.

3. Maybe I have been here before.
   I know this room; I've walked this floor.
   I used to live alone before I knew you.
   I've seen your flag on the marble arch.
   Love is not a victory march.
   It's a cold and it's a broken Hallelujah.

4. There was a time you let me know
   What's real and going on below.
   But now you never show it to me, do you?
   And remember when I moved in you,
   The holy dark was movin' too,
   And every breath we drew was Hallelujah.

5. Maybe there's a God above,
   And all I ever learned from love
   Was how to shoot at someone who outdrew you.
   And it's not a cry you can hear at night.
   It's not somebody who's seen the light.
   It's a cold and it's a broken Hallelujah.

GHOSTBUSTERS

from the Columbia Motion Picture GHOSTBUSTERS

Words and Music by
RAY PARKER, JR.

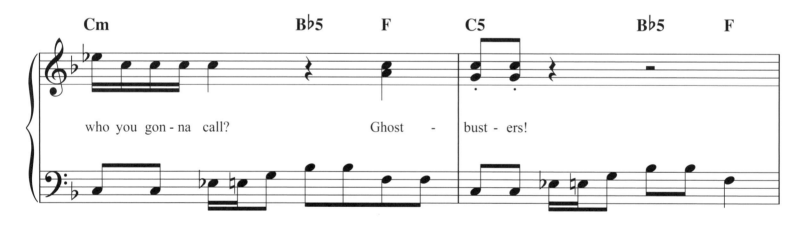

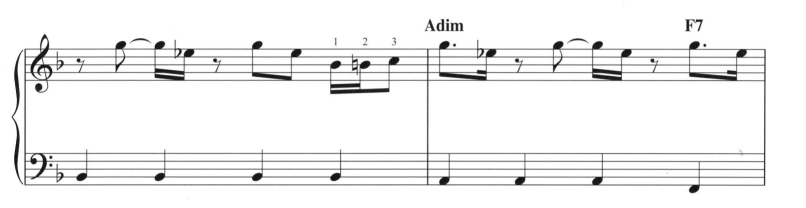

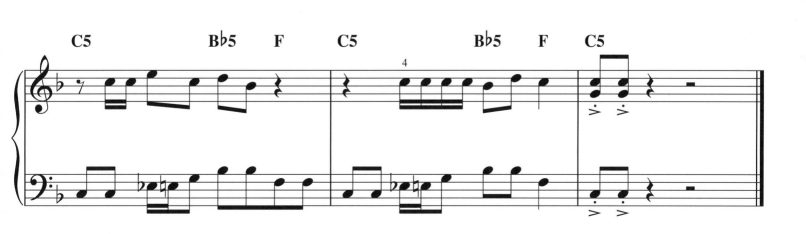

GLORY OF LOVE
Theme from KARATE KID PART II

Words and Music by DAVID FOSTER,
PETER CETERA and DIANE NINI

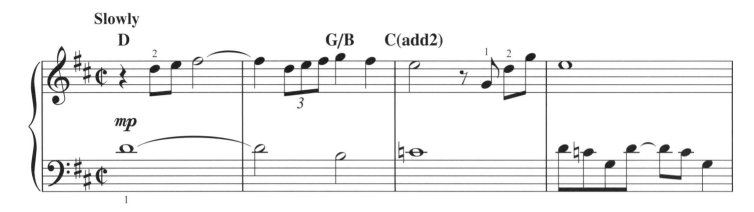

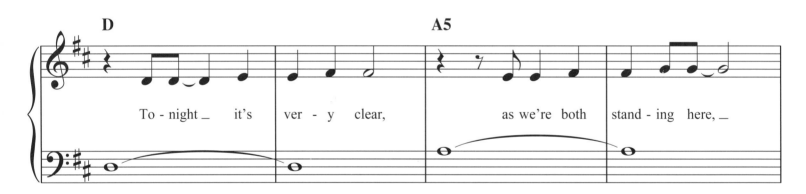

To - night ___ it's ver - y clear, as we're both stand - ing here, ___

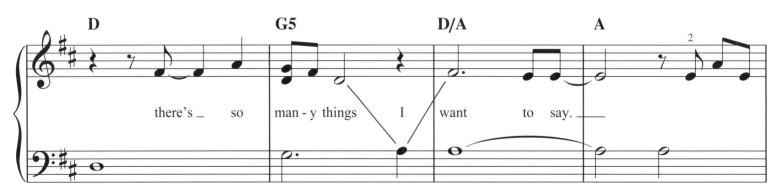

there's ___ so man - y things I want to say. ___

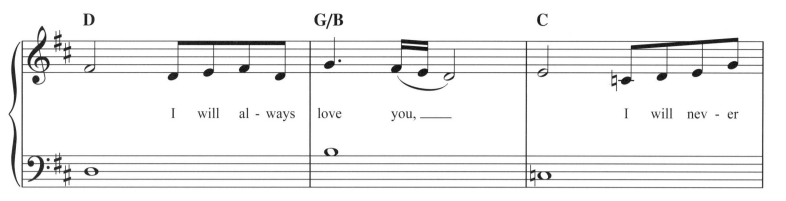

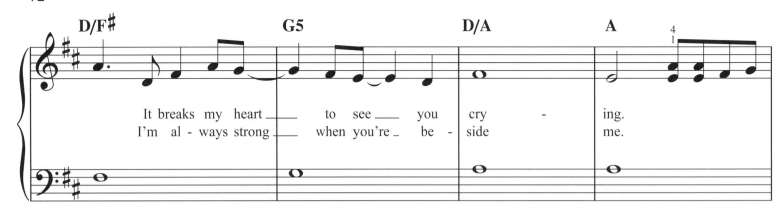

It breaks my heart ____ to see ____ you cry - ing.
I'm al - ways strong ____ when you're ____ be - side me.

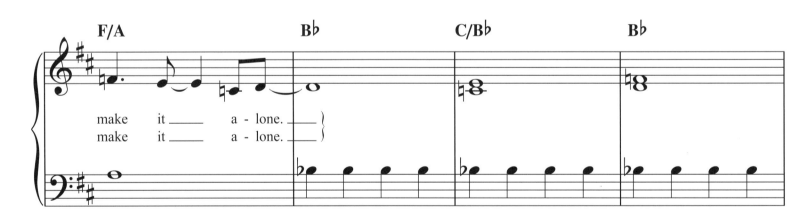

I don't want to lose you, ____ I could nev - er
I have al - ways need - ed ____ you, I could nev - er

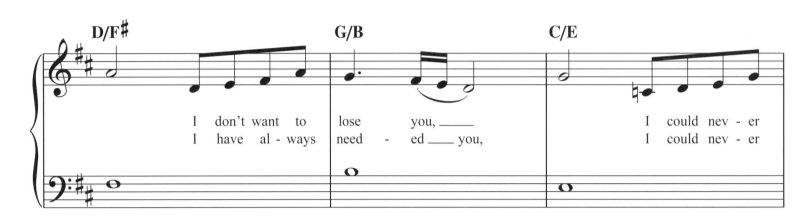

make it ____ a - lone. ____
make it ____ a - lone. ____

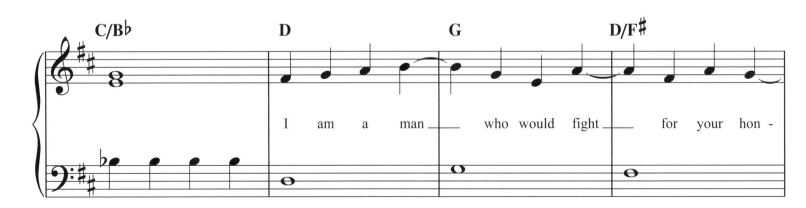

I am a man ____ who would fight ____ for your hon -

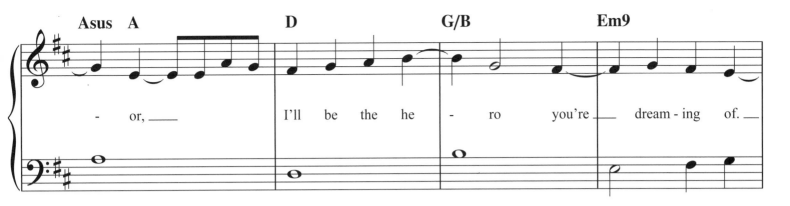

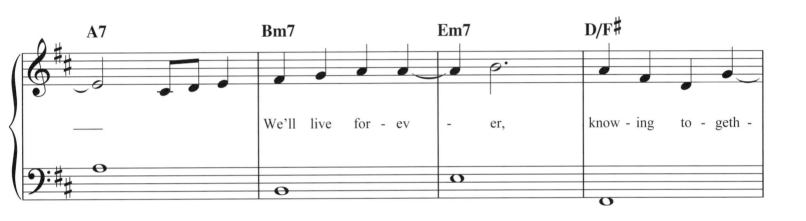

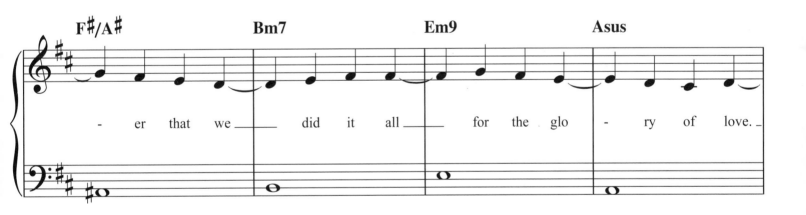

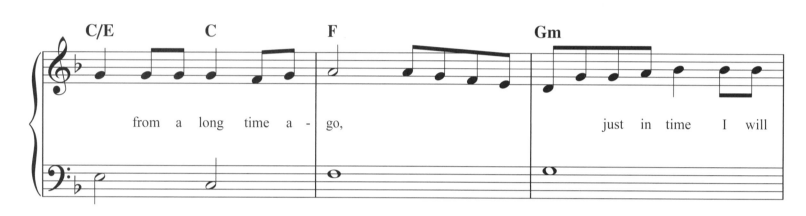

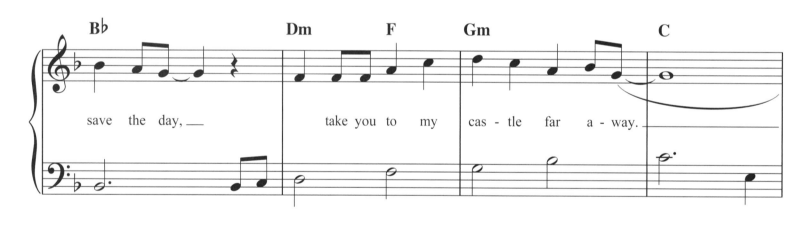

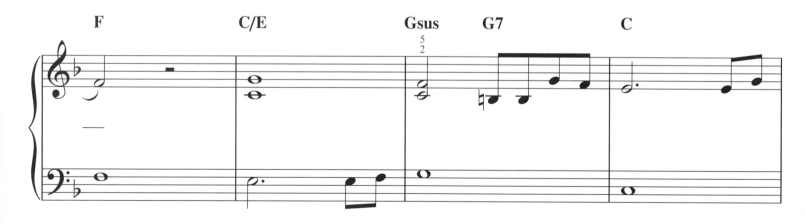

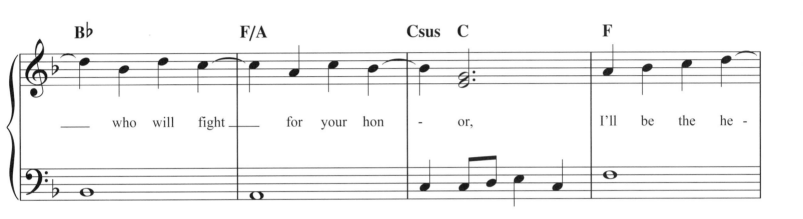

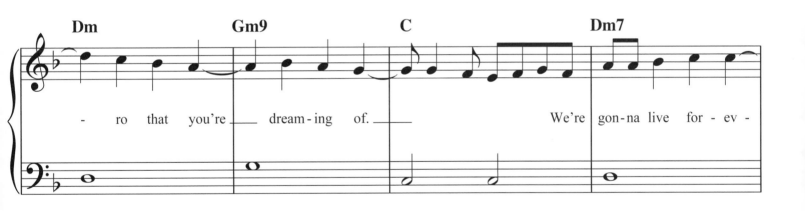

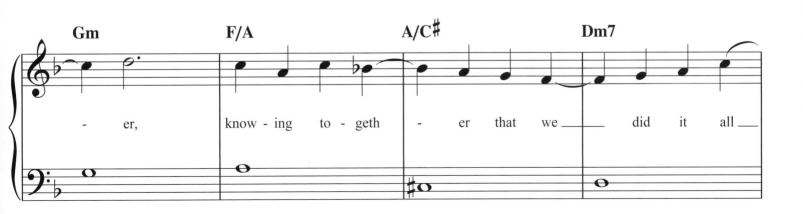

for the glo - ry of love.

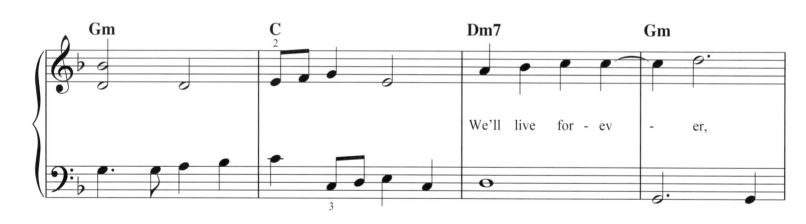

We'll live for - ev - er,

know - ing to - geth - er that we __ did it all __ for the glo -

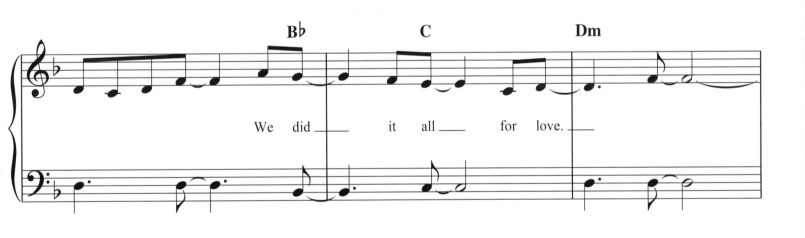

HAPPY
from DESPICABLE ME 2

Words and Music by
PHARRELL WILLIAMS

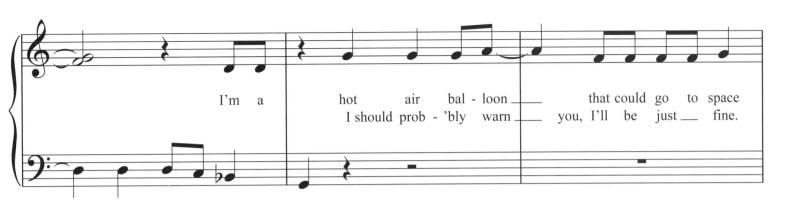

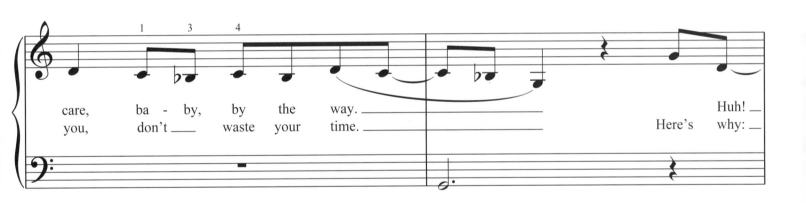

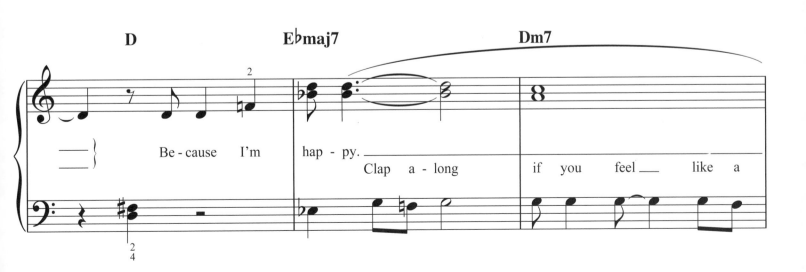

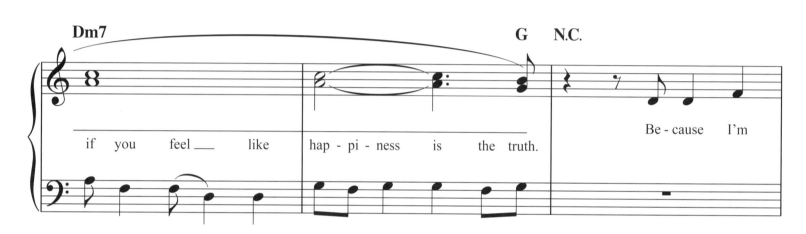

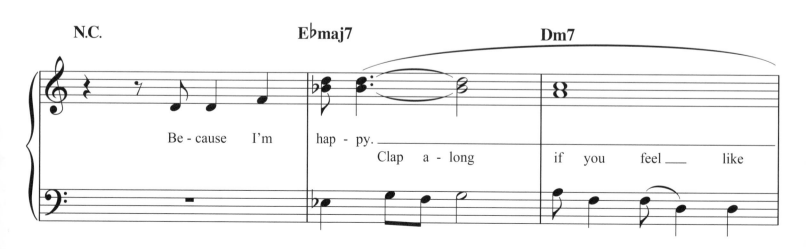

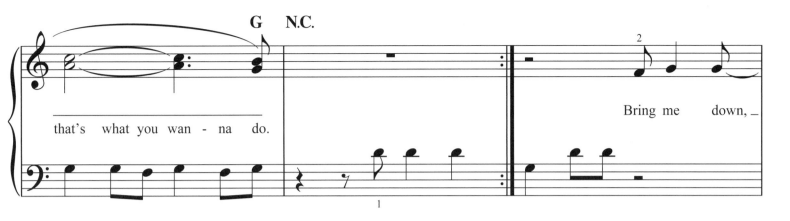

that's what you wan - na do.
Bring me down, _

_ can't noth - in' bring me down; _ your love is too

high. Bring me down, _ can't noth - in' bring me down. _

_ (Let me tell you now.) Bring me down, _ can't noth - in'

82

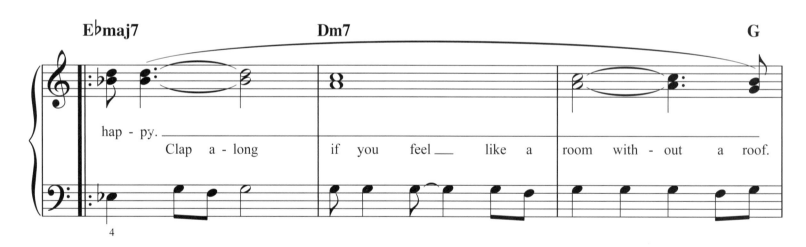

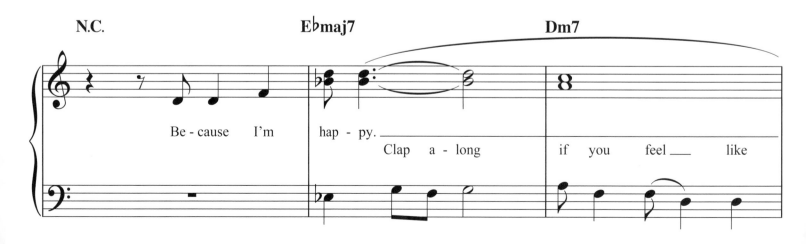

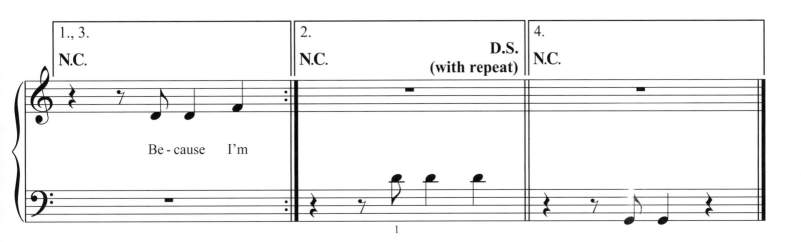

I BELIEVE I CAN FLY
from SPACE JAM

Words and Music by
ROBERT KELLY

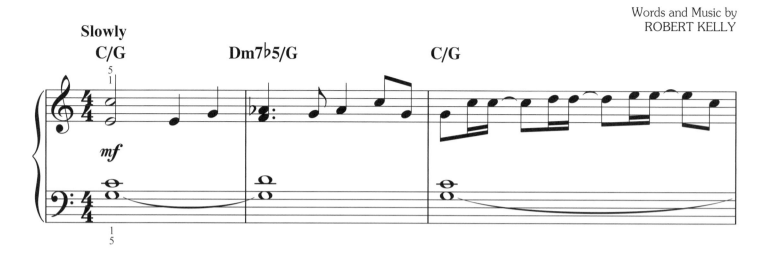

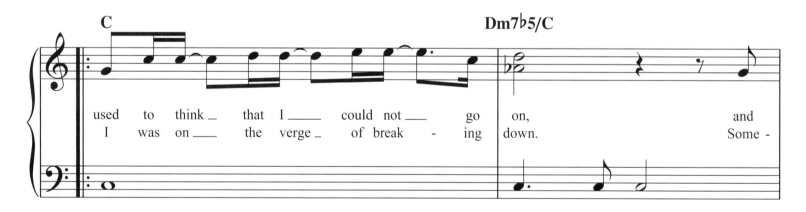

used to think _ that I ___ could not _ go on,   and
I was on _ the verge _ of break - ing down.   Some -

life was noth - ing but _ an aw - ful song. _____ But
times si - lence _ can seem _ so loud. _____ There are

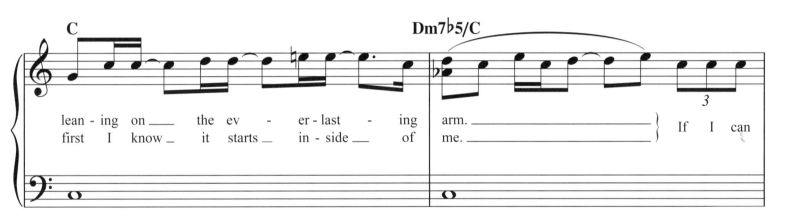

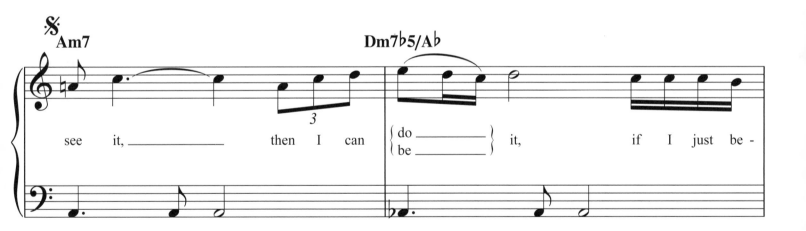

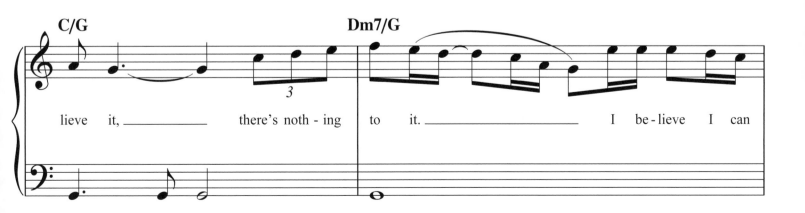

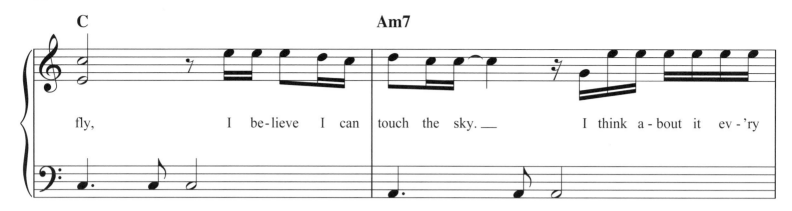

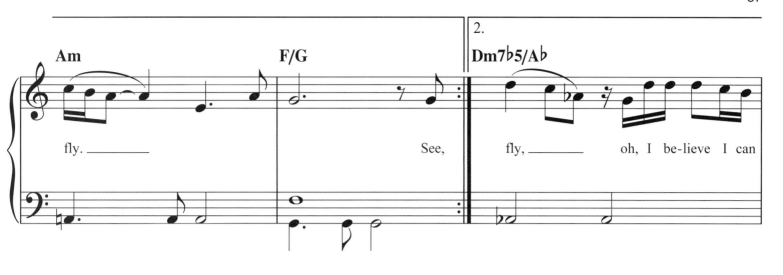

fly. _____ See, fly, _____ oh, I be-lieve I can

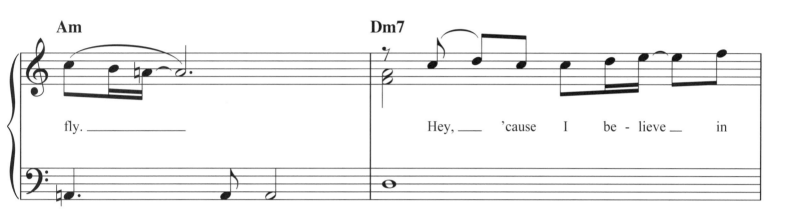

fly. _____ Hey, _____ 'cause I be-lieve _____ in

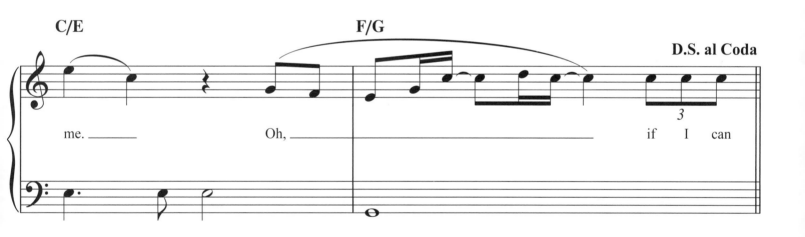

me. _____ Oh, _____ if I can

fly, I be-lieve I can fly, _____ I be-lieve I can

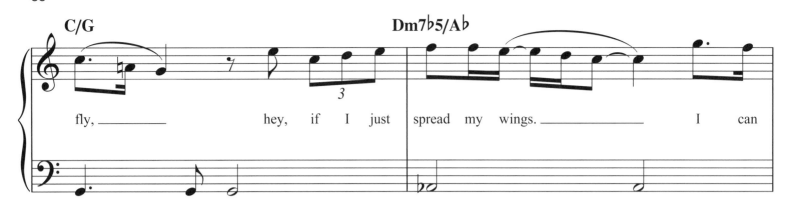

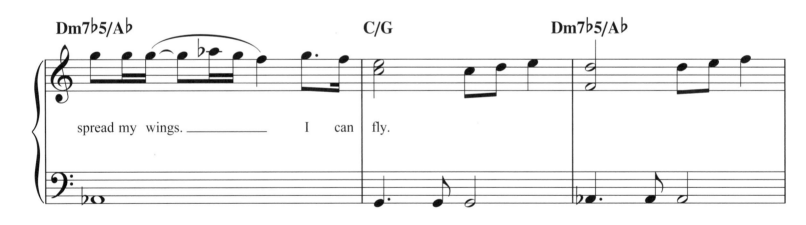

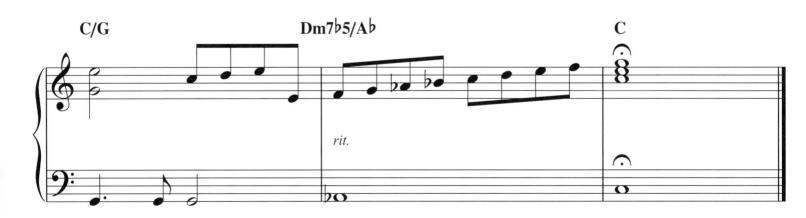

HOW DEEP IS YOUR LOVE

from the Motion Picture SATURDAY NIGHT FEVER

Words and Music by BARRY GIBB,
ROBIN GIBB and MAURICE GIBB

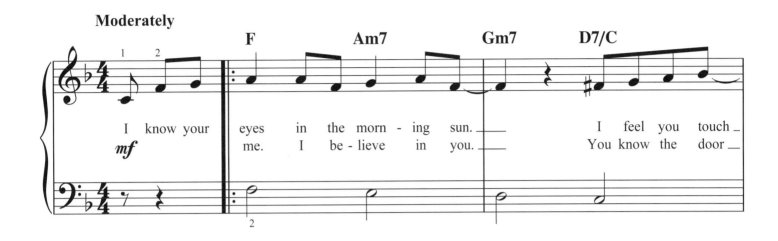

I know your eyes in the morn-ing sun. _ I feel you touch _
me. I be-lieve in you. _ You know the door _

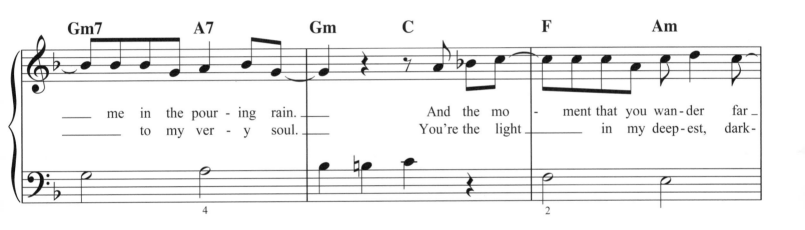

_ me in the pour-ing rain. _ And the mo - ment that you wan-der far _
_ to my ver - y soul. _ You're the light _ in my deep-est, dark-

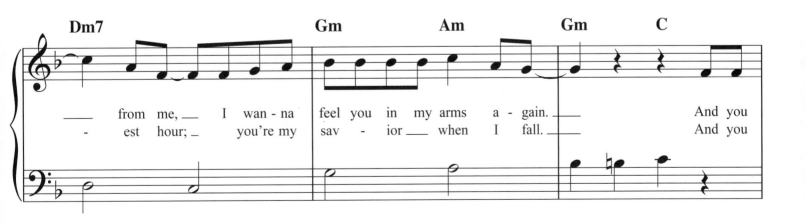

_ from me, _ I wan-na feel you in my arms a - gain. _ And you
- est hour; _ you're my sav - ior _ when I fall. _ And you

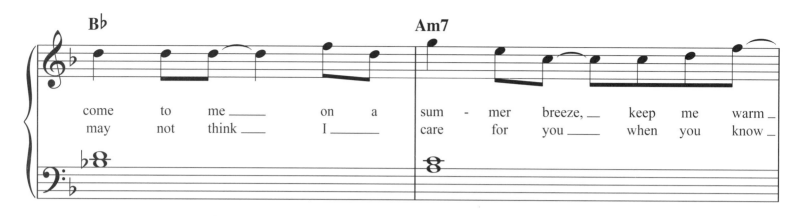

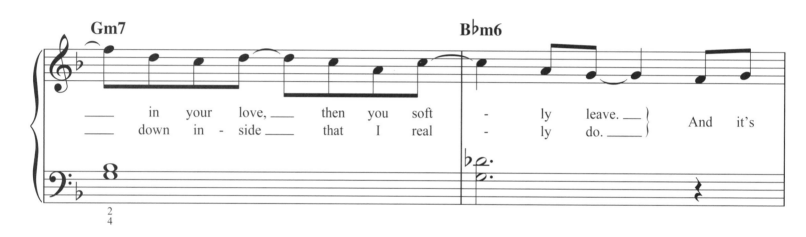

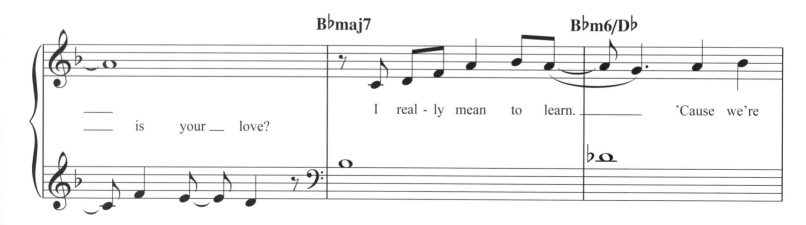

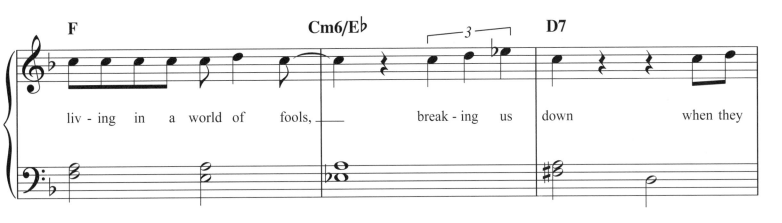

liv - ing in a world of fools, ___ break - ing us down when they

all should let us be. ___ We be - long ___ to you and

me.

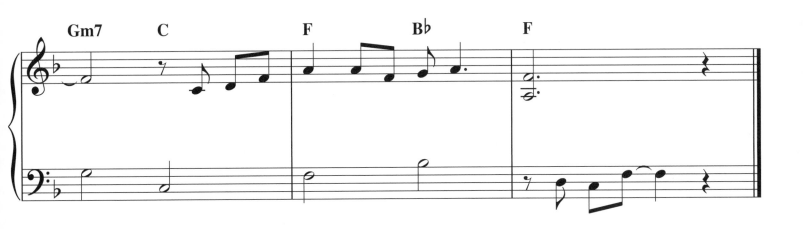

LA BAMBA

featured in the Motion Picture LA BAMBA

By RITCHIE VALENS

Moderate Latin rhythm

Pa - ra bai - lar la bam - ba.

Pa - ra bai - lar la bam - ba se ne - ce - si - ta un po - ca de

gra - cia. Un - a po - ca de gra - cia para mi para ti

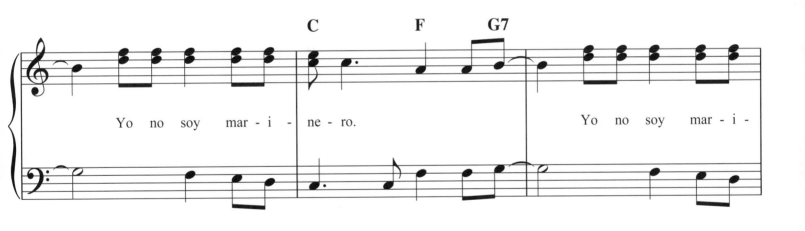

y ar - ri - ba ar - ri - ba;   ar - ri - ba ar -

ri - ba por ti se re   por ti se re se - re.

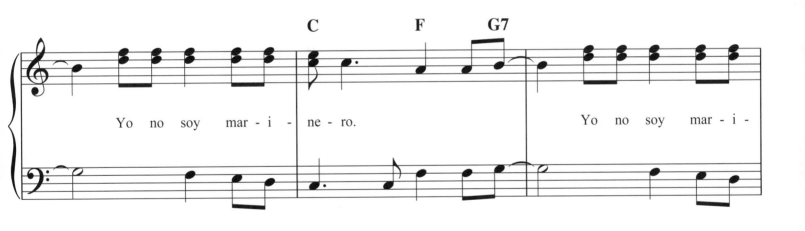

Yo no soy mar - i - ne - ro.   Yo no soy mar - i -

ne - ro, soy cap - i - tan;   yo no soy mar - i - ne - ro, soy cap - i - tan.

94

I JUST CALLED TO SAY I LOVE YOU
from THE WOMAN IN RED

Words and Music by
STEVIE WONDER

Chorus

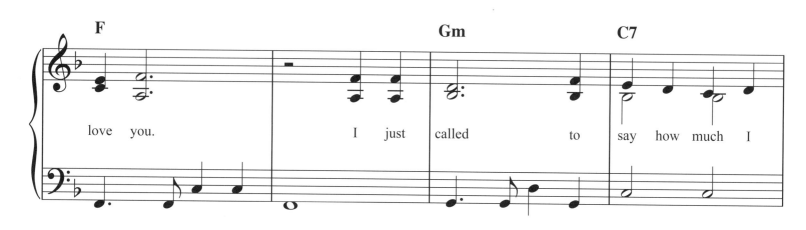

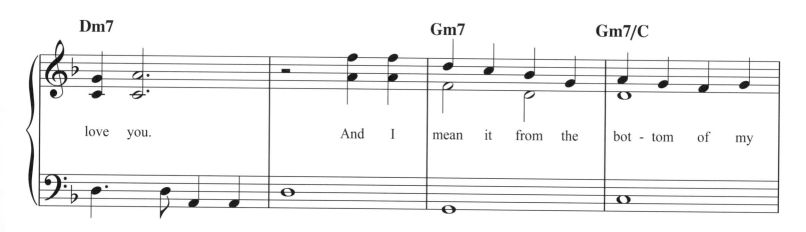

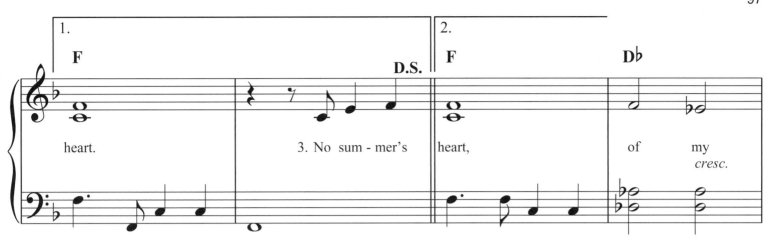

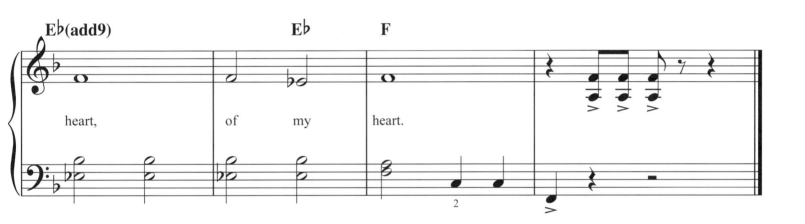

Additional Lyrics

2. No April rain; no flowers bloom;
   No wedding Saturday within the month of June.
   But what it is, is something true,
   Made up of these three words that I must say to you.
   Chorus

3. No summer's high; no warm July;
   No harvest moon to light one tender August night.
   No autumn breeze; no falling leaves;
   Not even time for birds to fly to southern skies.

4. No Libra sun; no Halloween;
   No giving thanks to all the Christmas joy you bring.
   But what it is, though old, so new
   To fill your heart like no three words could ever do.
   Chorus

I WILL ALWAYS LOVE YOU

featured in THE BODYGUARD

Words and Music by
DOLLY PARTON

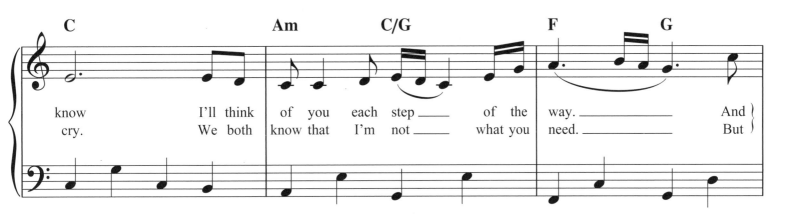

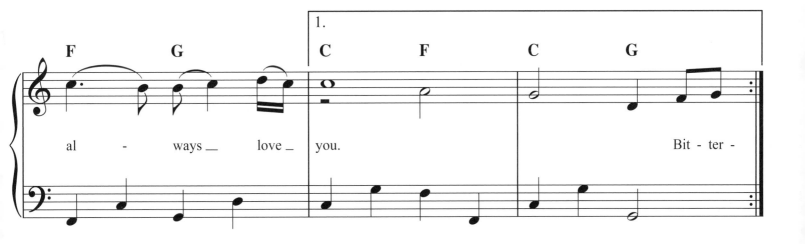

LET IT GO
from Disney's Animated Feature FROZEN

Music and Lyrics by KRISTEN ANDERSON-LOPEZ
and ROBERT LOPEZ

Half-time feel, mysterious

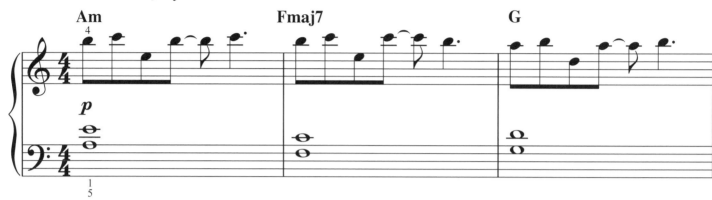

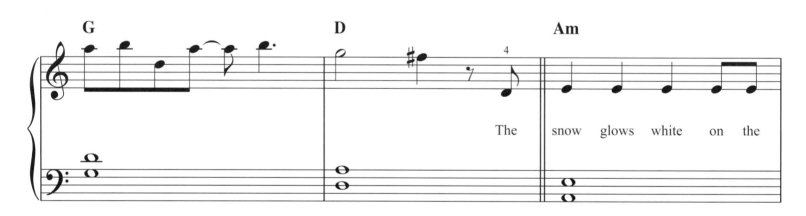

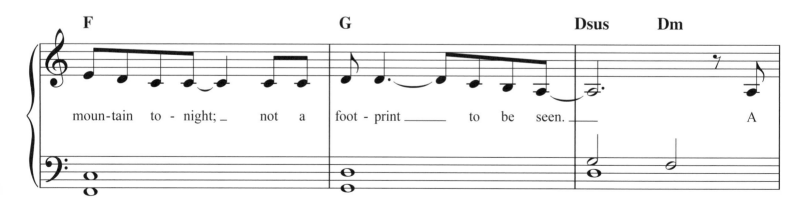

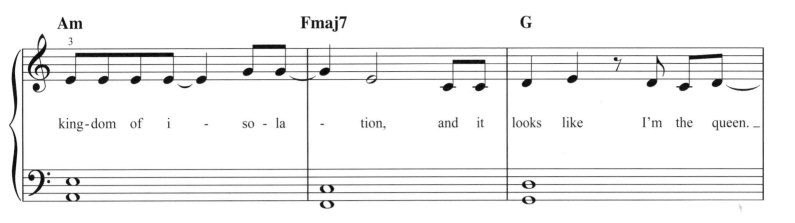

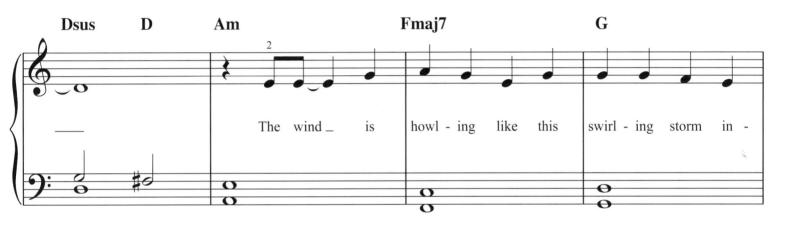

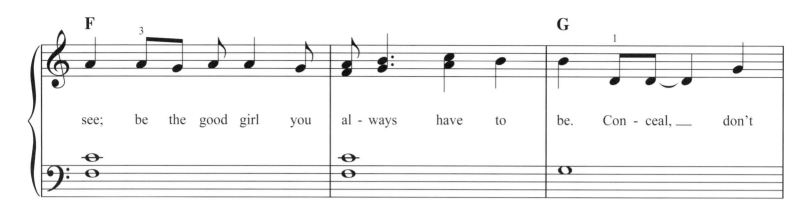

see; be the good girl you al - ways have to be. Con - ceal, __ don't

feel, don't let __ them know...   Well, now _

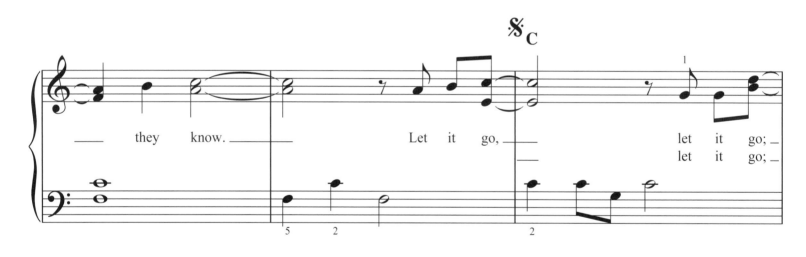

_ they know. ___ Let it go, ___ let it go; _
                                                         let it go; _

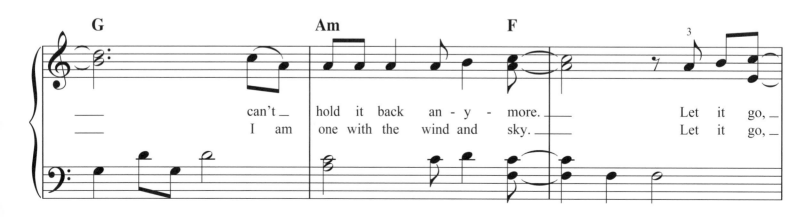

_ can't _ hold it back an - y - more. __ Let it go, _
_ I am one with the wind and sky. _ Let it go, _

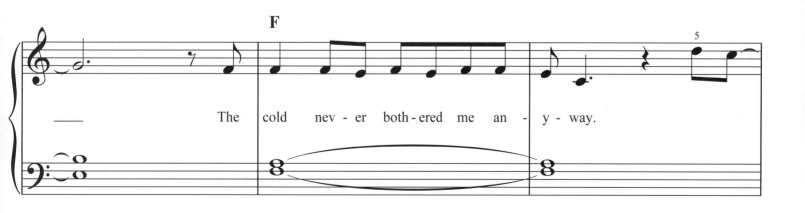

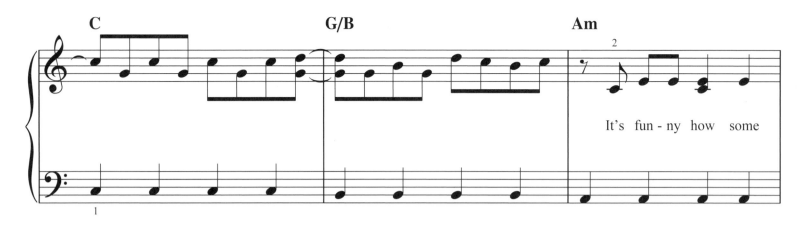

C   G/B   Am

It's fun - ny how some

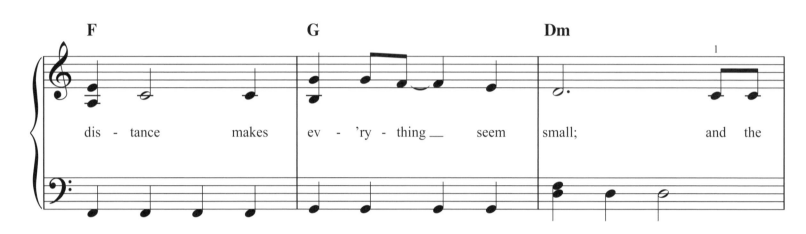

F   G   Dm

dis - tance makes ev - 'ry - thing ___ seem small;   and the

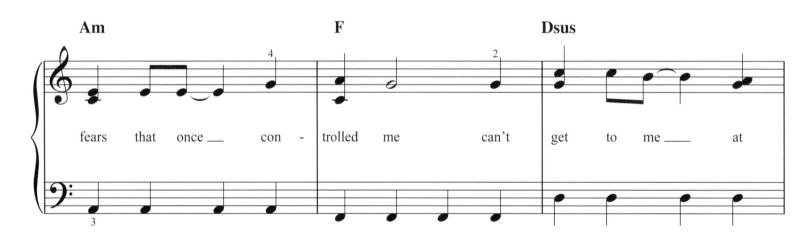

Am   F   Dsus

fears that once ___ con - trolled me can't get to me ___ at

D   G

all.   It's time ___ to see what I can

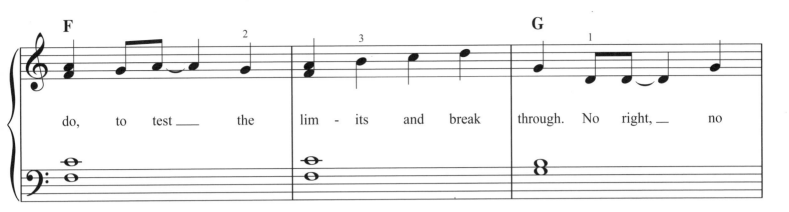

do, to test ___ the lim - its and break through. No right, ___ no

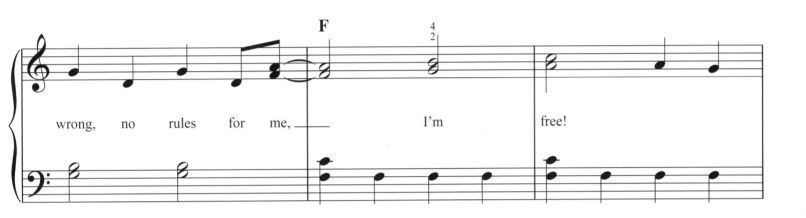

wrong, no rules for me, ___ I'm free!

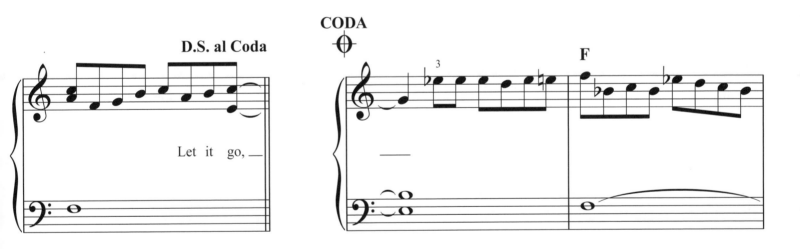

D.S. al Coda

CODA

Let it go, ___ ___

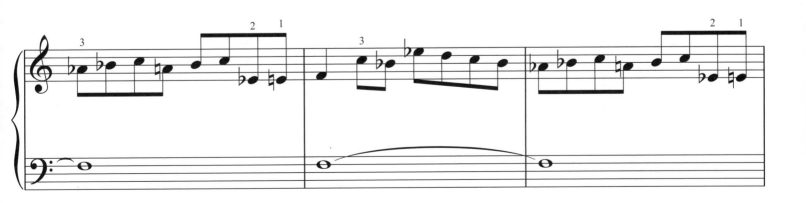

106

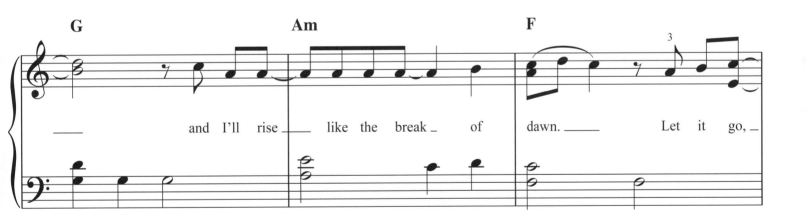

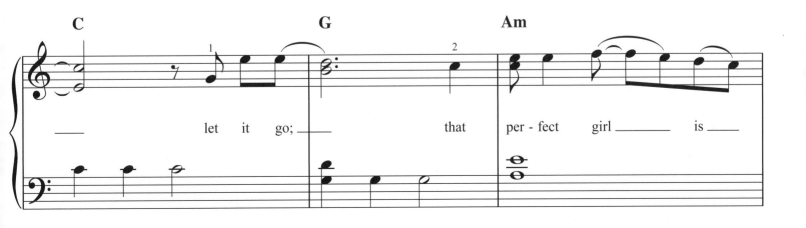

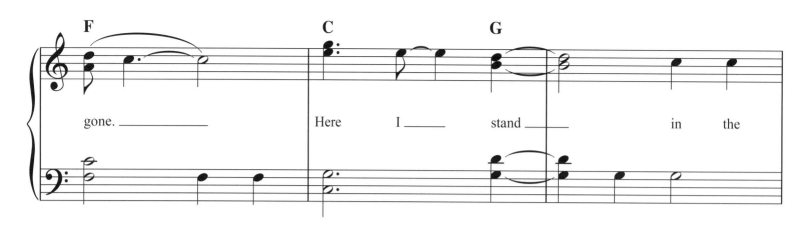

gone. _____ Here I _____ stand _____ in the

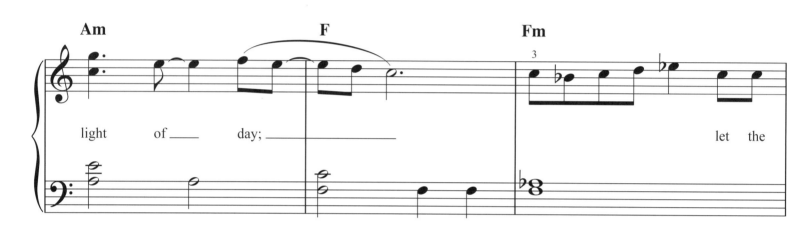

light of ___ day; _____ let the

storm rage ___ on. _____ The

cold nev - er both - ered me an - y - way. _____

LIVE AND LET DIE
from LIVE AND LET DIE

Words and Music by PAUL McCARTNEY
and LINDA McCARTNEY

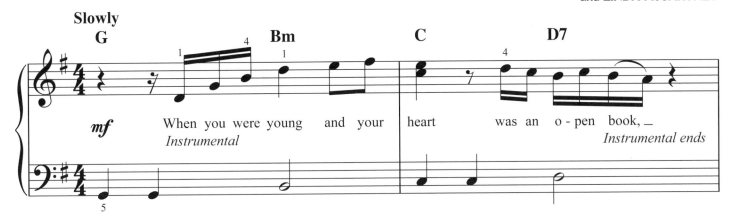

When you were young and your heart was an o-pen book, ___
Instrumental   *Instrumental ends*

you used to say   live and let   live.⎫
You used to say   live and let   live.⎭   (You know you did, you know you did, you know you

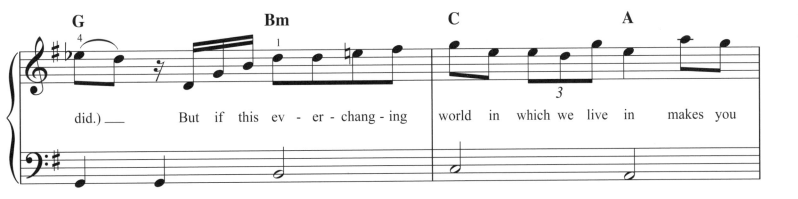

did.) ___   But if this ev-er-chang-ing   world in which we live in   makes you

give in and cry, ___   say live and let   die! ___   Live and let

die, _____ live and let die, _____ live and let die. _____

Instrumental

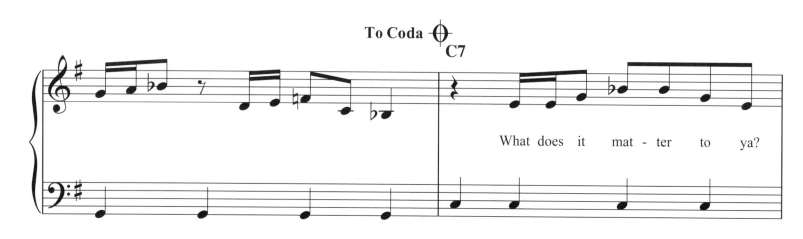

To Coda ⊕

What does it mat - ter to ya?

When you got a job to do, you got - ta do it well. You got - ta

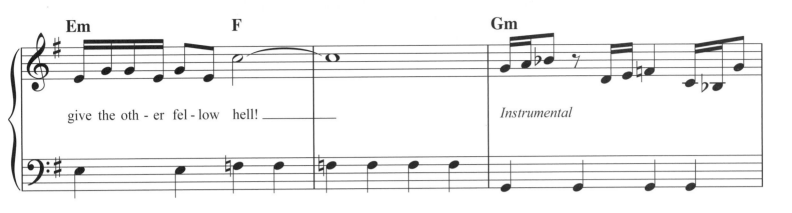

give the oth - er fel - low hell! _____

Instrumental

D.C. al Coda

CODA

Ebm/Gb

MRS. ROBINSON

from THE GRADUATE

Words and Music by
PAUL SIMON

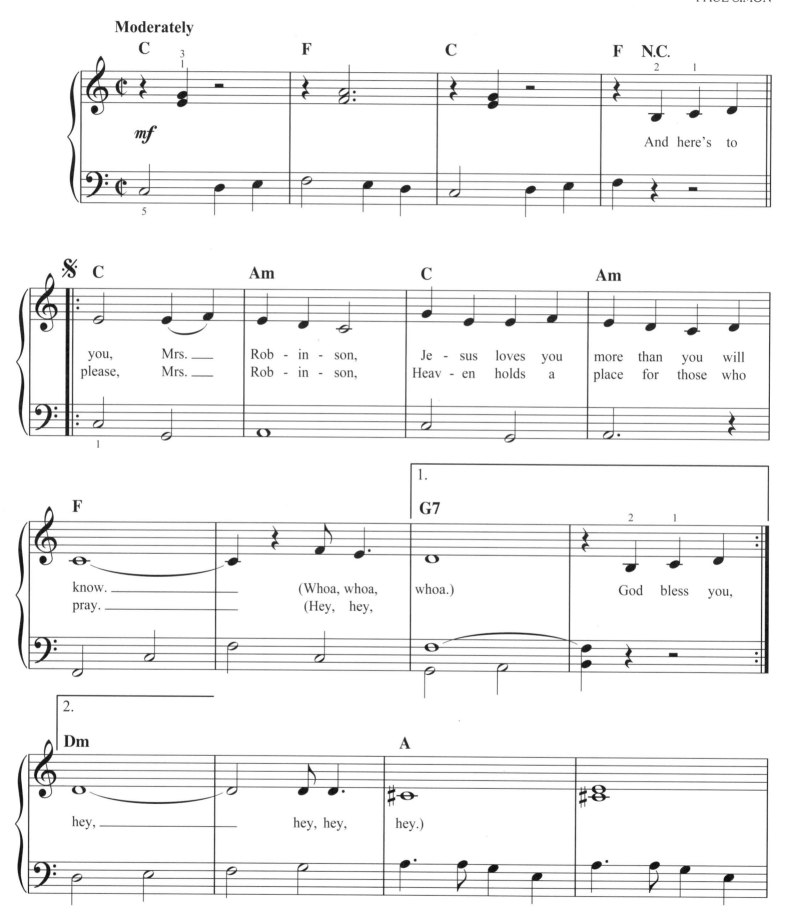

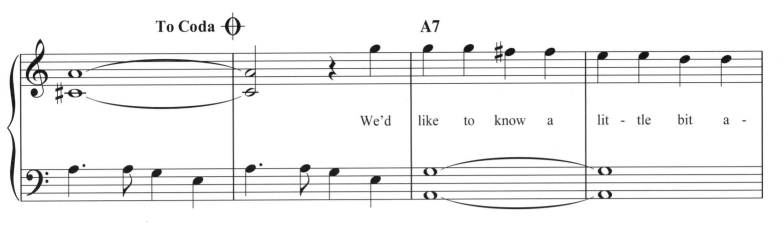

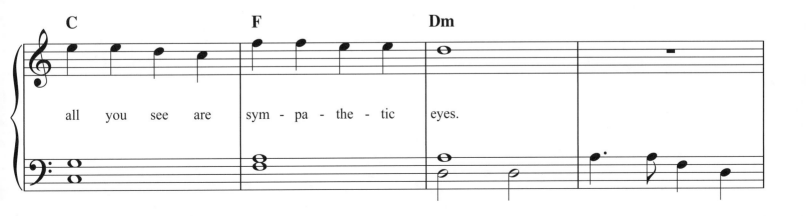

114

D.S. al Coda
(with repeat)

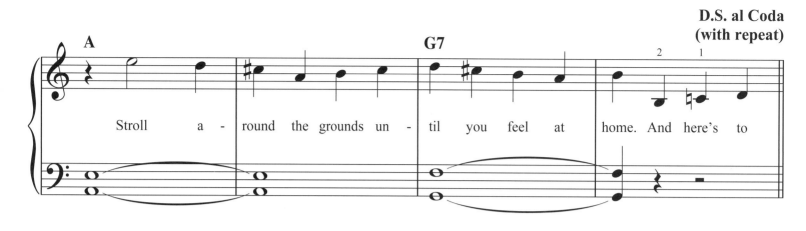

Stroll a - round the grounds un - til you feel at home. And here's to

CODA

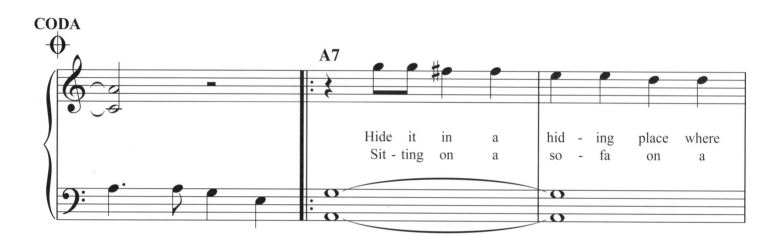

Hide it in a hid - ing place where
Sit - ting on a so - fa on a

no one ev - er goes, put it in your
Sun - day af - ter - noon, go - ing to the

pan - try with your cup - cakes. It's a lit - tle
can - di - date's de - bate. Laugh a - bout it,

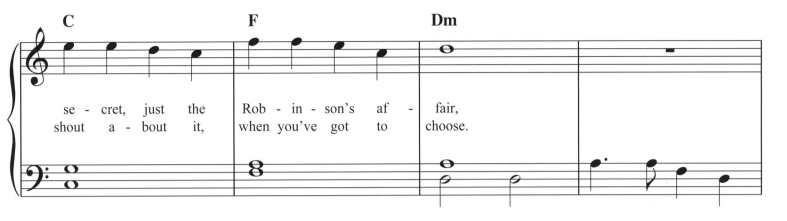

se - cret, just the | Rob - in - son's af - fair,
shout a - bout it, | when you've got to | choose.

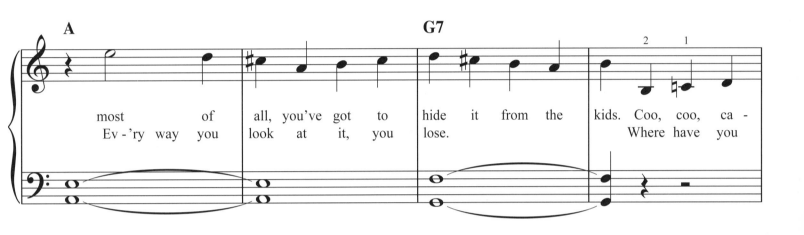

most of | all, you've got to | hide it from the | kids. Coo, coo, ca -
Ev - 'ry way you | look at it, you | lose. | Where have you

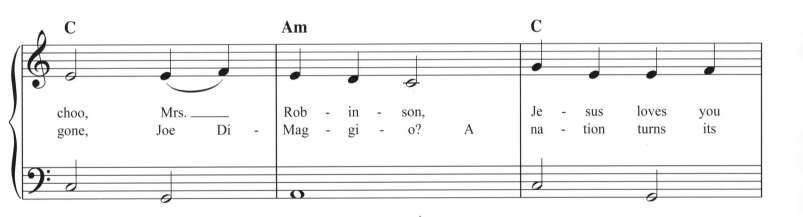

choo, Mrs. _____ | Rob - in - son, | Je - sus loves you
gone, Joe Di - | Mag - gi - o? A | na - tion turns its

more than you will | know. _____ | (Whoa, whoa, | whoa.)
lone - ly eyes to | you. _____ | (Woo, woo, | woo.)

God bless you, please, Mrs. _____ Rob - in - son,
What's that you say, Mrs. _____ Rob - in - son,

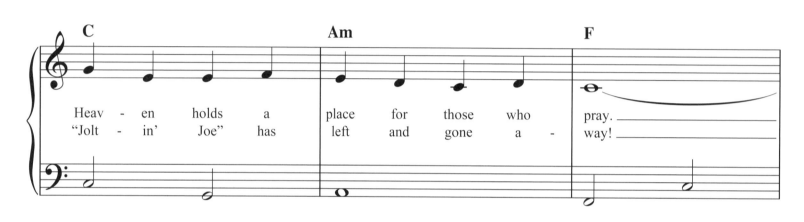

Heav - en holds a place for those who pray. _____
"Jolt - in' Joe" has left and gone a - way! _____

_____ (Hey, hey, hey, _____ hey, hey, hey.)
_____ (Hey, hey, hey, _____ hey, hey, hey.)

MOON RIVER
from the Paramount Picture BREAKFAST AT TIFFANY'S

Words by JOHNNY MERCER
Music by HENRY MANCINI

Slowly and expressively

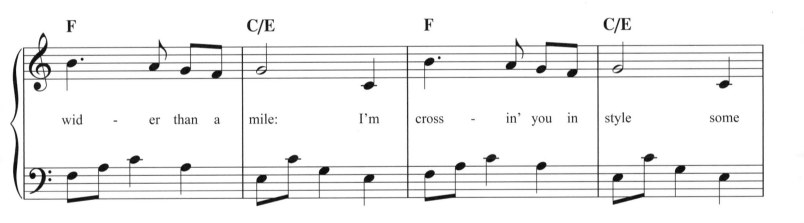

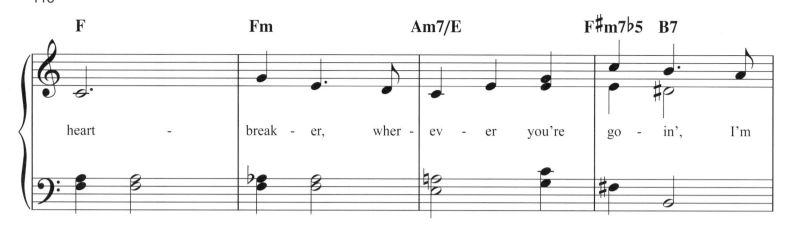

F **Fm** **Am7/E** **F#m7b5** **B7**

heart - break - er, wher - ev - er you're go - in', I'm

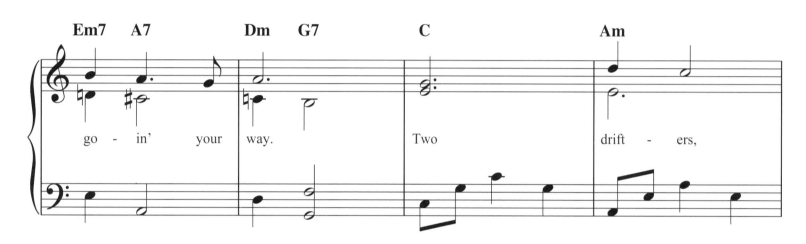

Em7 **A7** **Dm** **G7** **C** **Am**

go - in' your way. Two drift - ers,

F **C/E** **F** **C/E**

off to see the world. There's such a lot of world to

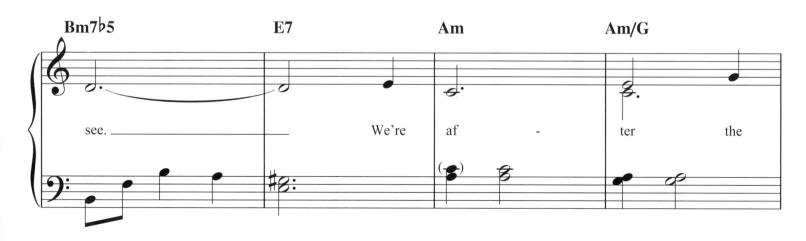

Bm7b5 **E7** **Am** **Am/G**

see. _____ We're af - ter the

MY HEART WILL GO ON
(Love Theme from 'Titanic')
from the Paramount and Twentieth Century Fox Motion Picture TITANIC

Music by JAMES HORNER
Lyric by WILL JENNINGS

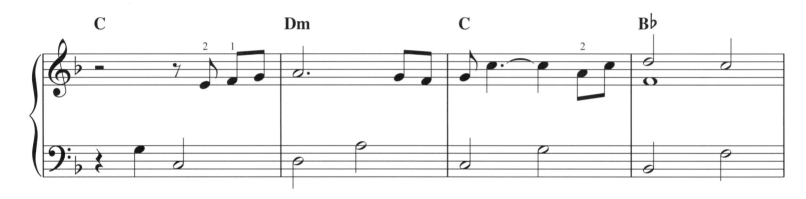

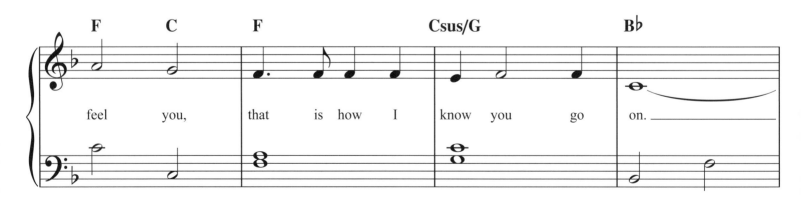

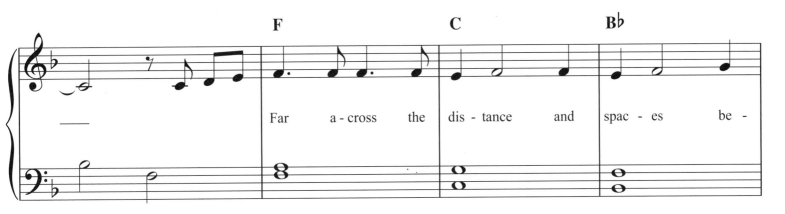

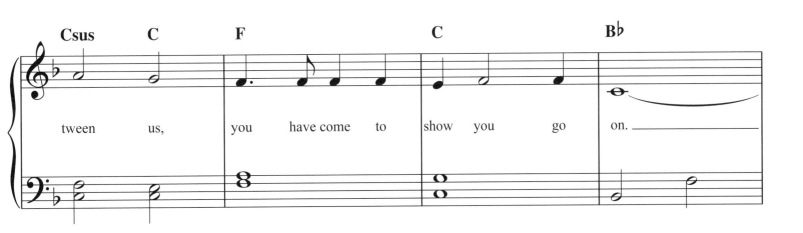

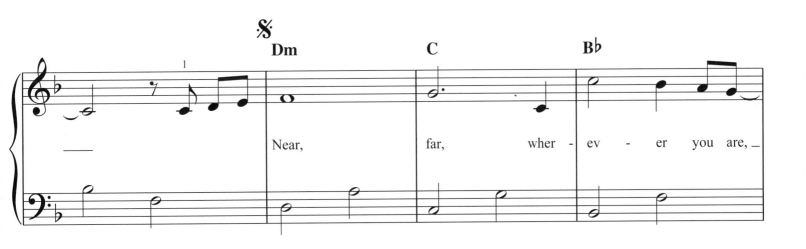

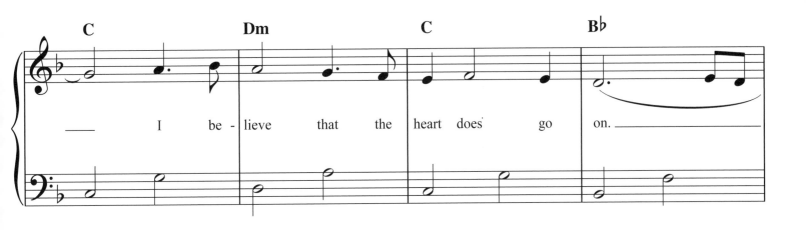

122

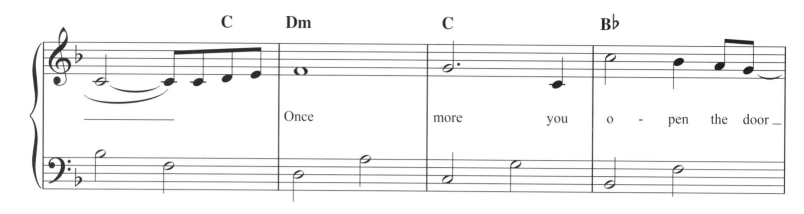

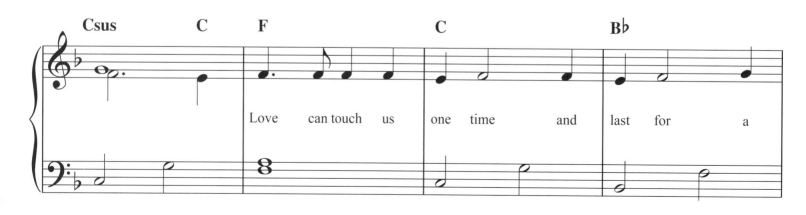

123

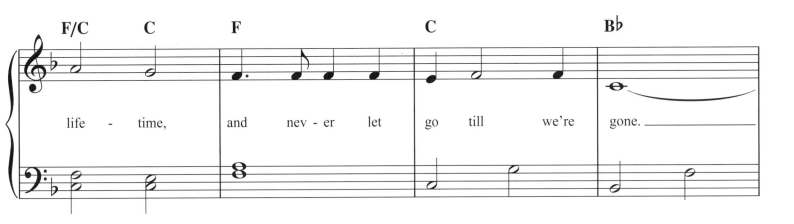

life - time, and nev-er let go till we're gone. _____

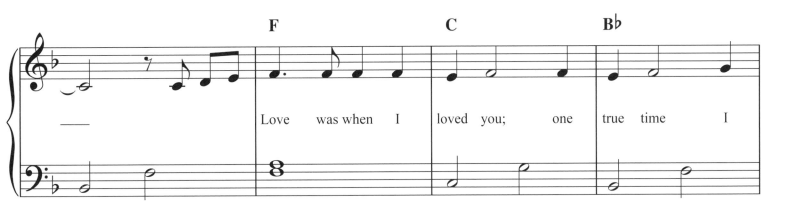

_____ Love was when I loved you; one true time I

hold to. In my life we'll al - ways go on. _____

D.S. al Coda

CODA

on.

124

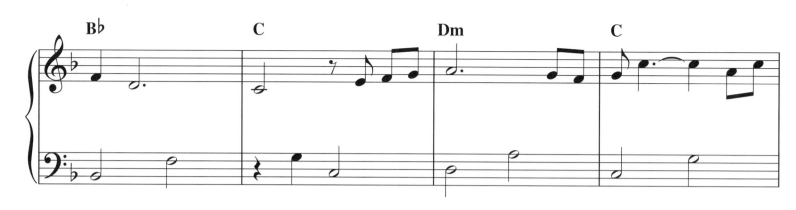

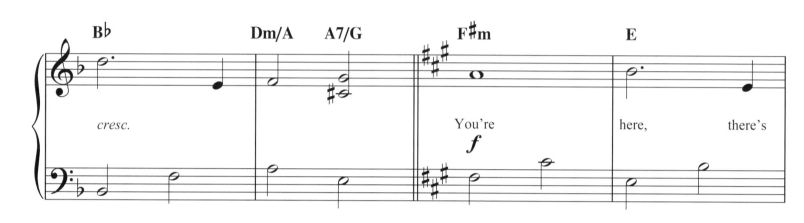

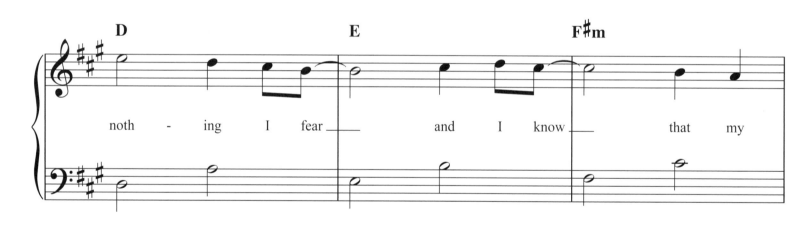

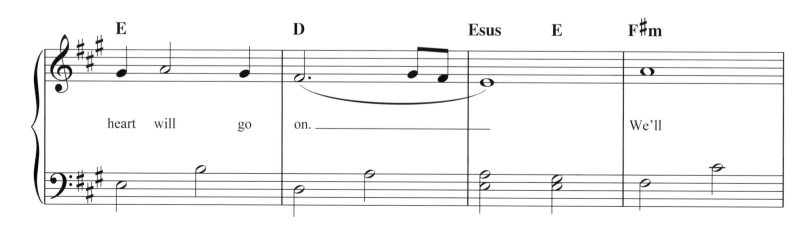

125

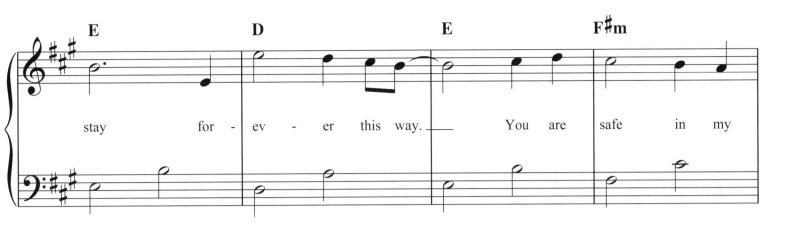

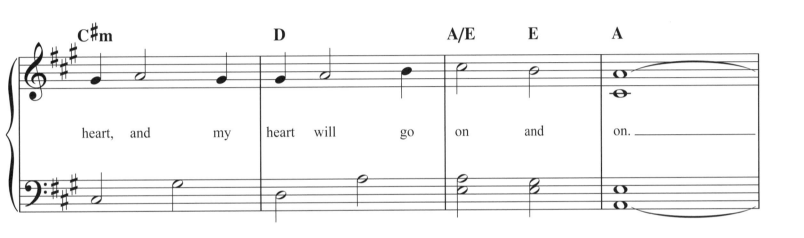

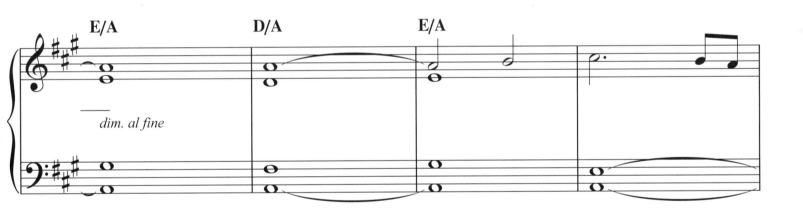

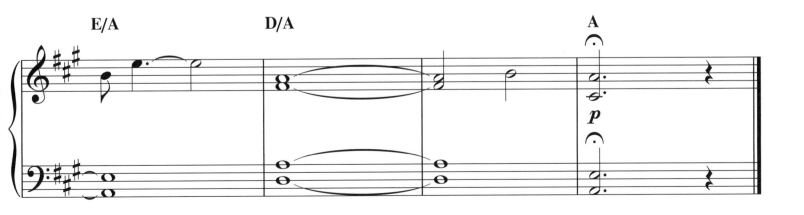

NIGHT FEVER
from SATURDAY NIGHT FEVER

Words and Music by BARRY GIBB,
ROBIN GIBB and MAURICE GIBB

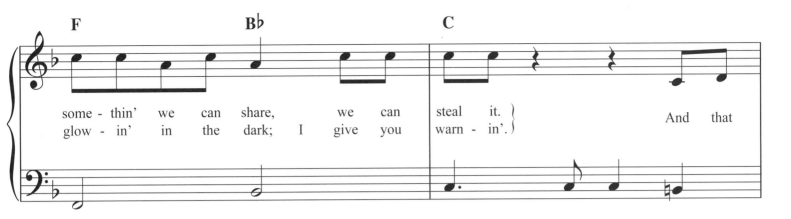

F   B♭   C

some - thin' we can share,   we can   steal it.   And that
glow - in' in the dark; I give you   warn - in'.

Am   B♭

sweet cit - y wom - an, she   moves through the light, _____ con -

Am   Em

trol - ling my mind __ and my   soul. _____ When you

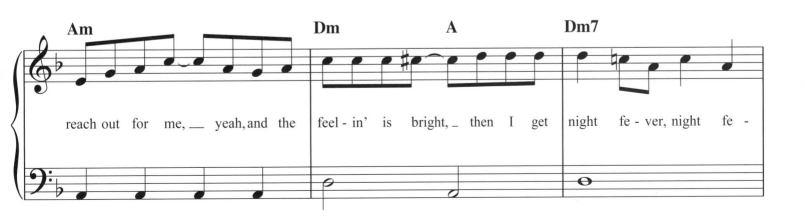

Am   Dm   A   Dm7

reach out for me, __ yeah, and the   feel - in' is bright, _ then I get   night fe - ver, night fe -

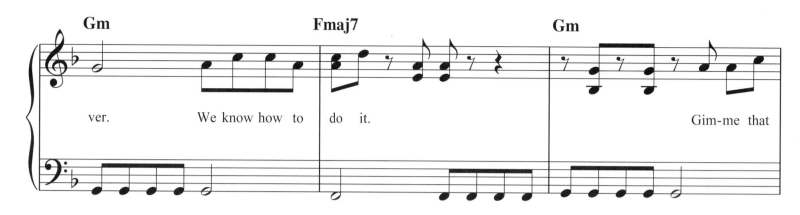

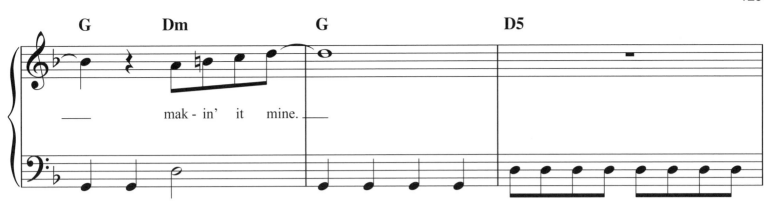

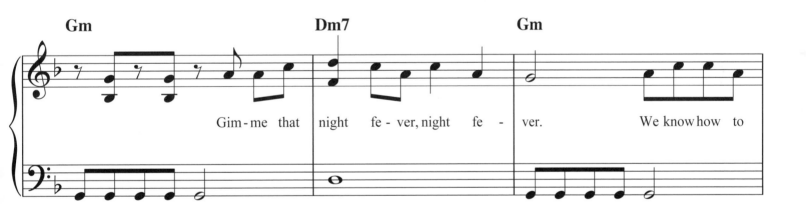

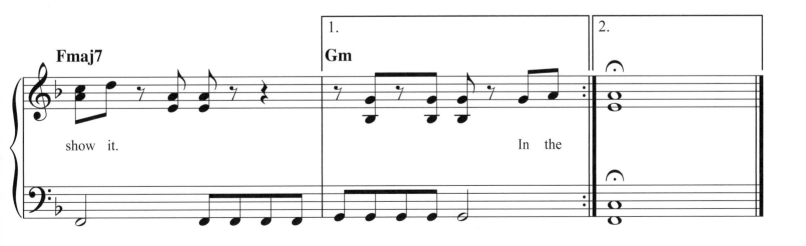

OVER THE RAINBOW
from THE WIZARD OF OZ

Music by HAROLD ARLEN
Lyric by E.Y. "YIP" HARBURG

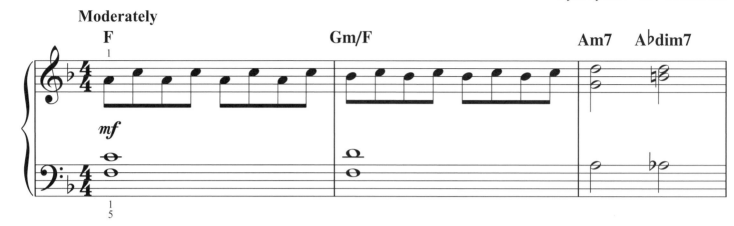

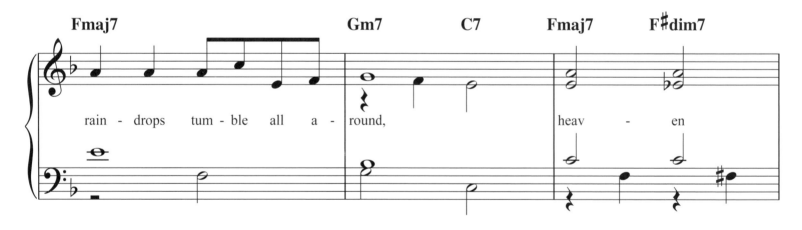

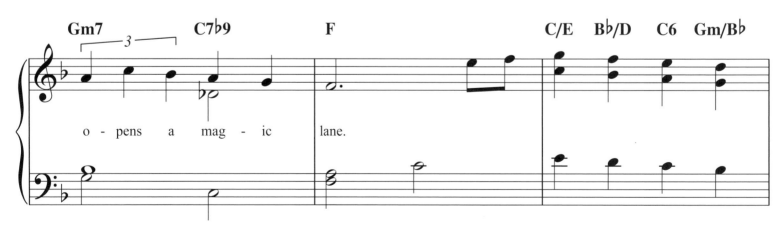

When all the clouds dark - en up the sky - way, there's a rain - bow high - way to be

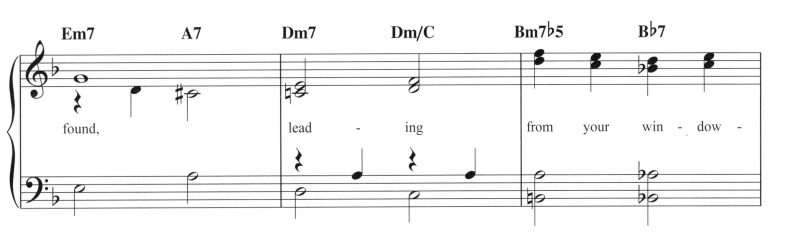

found, lead - ing from your win - dow -

pane _____ to a place be - hind the sun, _____

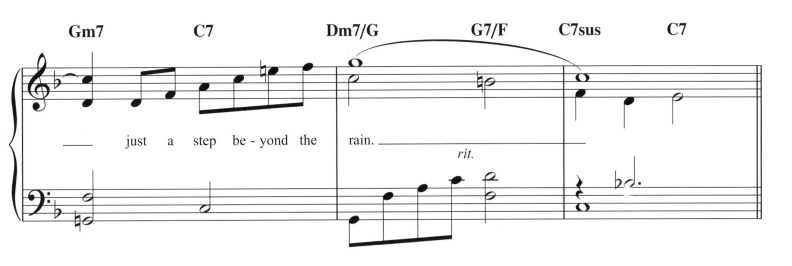

_____ just a step be - yond the rain. _____ *rit.*

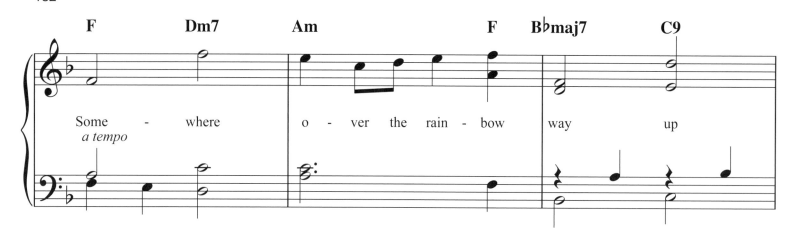

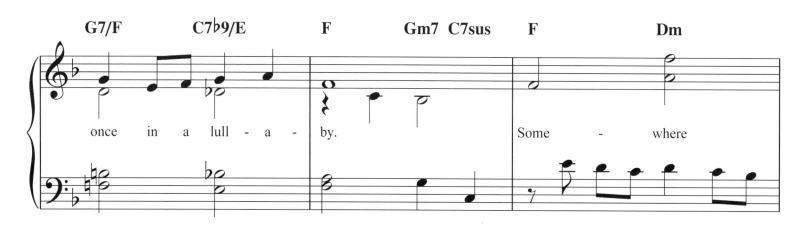

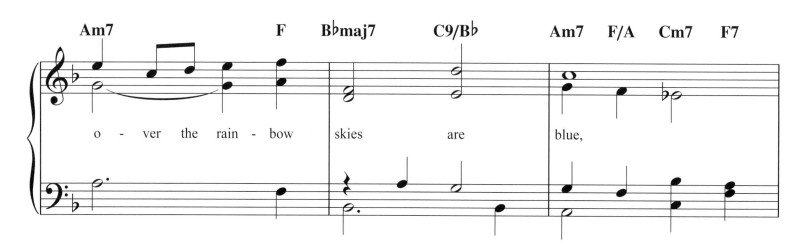

and the dreams that you dare to dream real - ly do come

true. _____ Some - day I'll wish up - on a star and wake up where the clouds are far be -

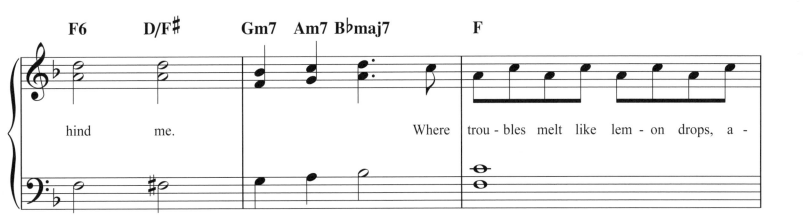

hind me. Where trou - bles melt like lem - on drops, a -

way, a - bove the chim - ney tops that's where you'll find me.

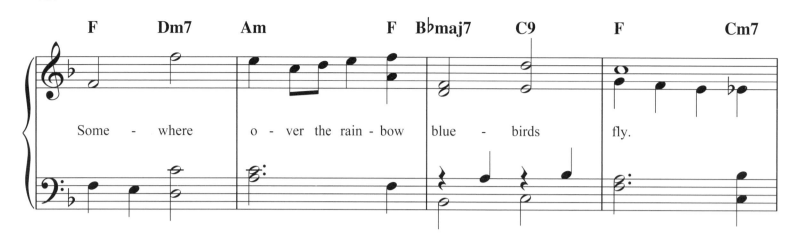

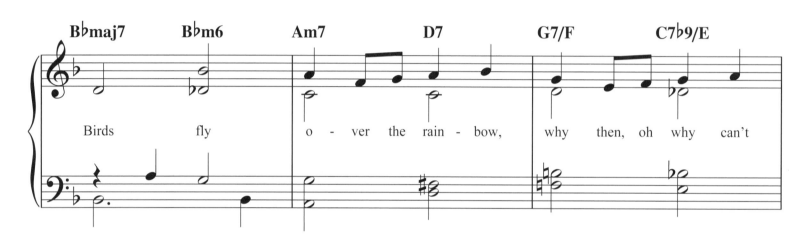

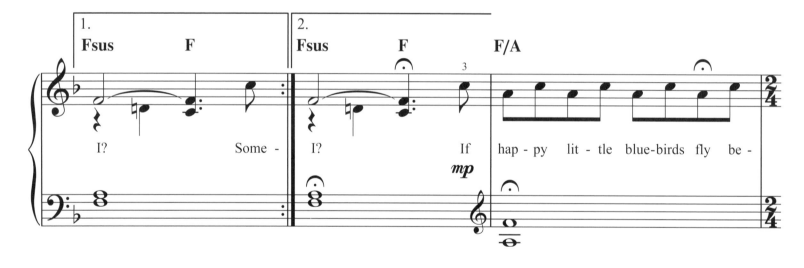

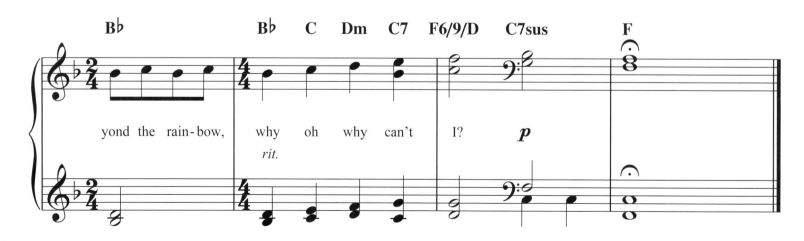

NINE TO FIVE

from NINE TO FIVE

Words and Music by
DOLLY PARTON

Tum - ble out of bed and stum - ble to the kitch - en;
They let you dream just to watch _ them _ shat - ter;

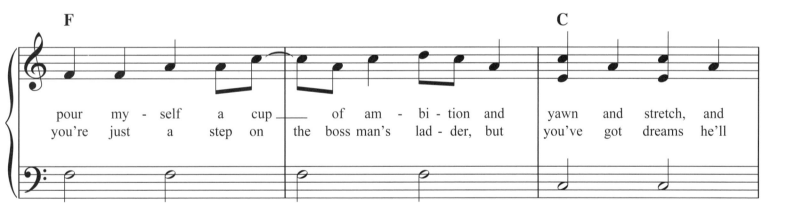

pour my - self a cup _ of am - bi - tion and yawn and stretch, and
you're just a step on the boss man's lad - der, but you've got dreams he'll

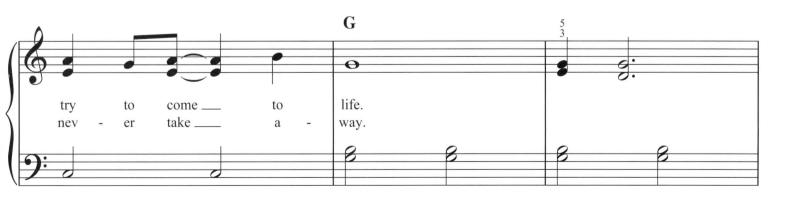

try to come _ to life.
nev - er take _ a - way.

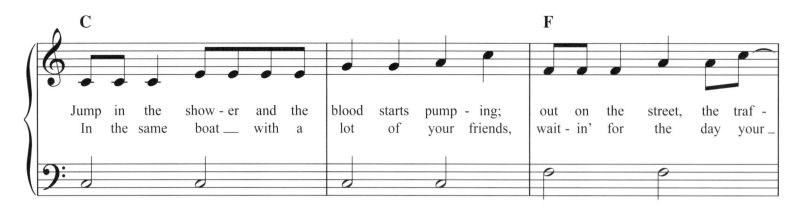

C .... **F**

Jump in the show - er and the blood starts pump - ing; out on the street, the traf -
In the same boat __ with a lot of your friends, wait - in' for the day your __

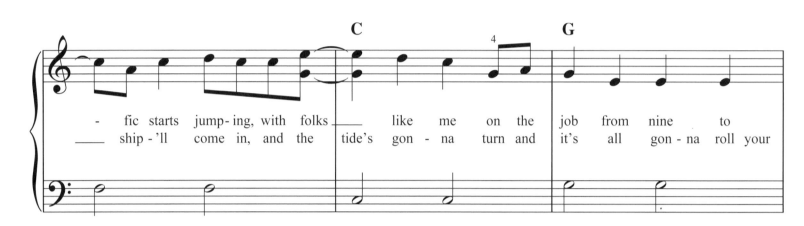

C .... **G**

- fic starts jump - ing, with folks __ like me on the job from nine to
__ ship - 'll come in, and the tide's gon - na turn and it's all gon - na roll your

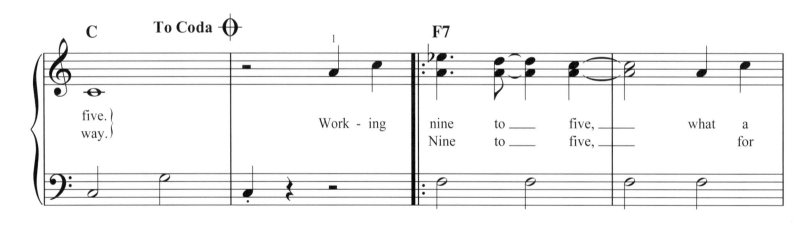

C To Coda ⊕ **F7**

five. }
way. }   Work - ing nine to __ five, __ what a
                                 Nine to __ five, __ what for

.... **C**

way to make __ a liv - ing; bare - ly get - ting
ser - vice and __ de - vo - tion; you would think __ that

by,   it's   all   tak - ing and ___ no   giv - ing. They just
I   would de - serve a fair ___ pro - mo - tion. Want to

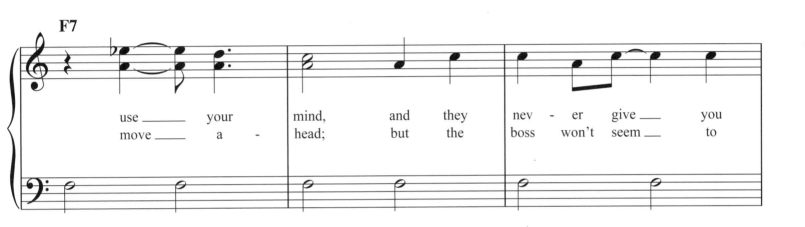

F7

use ___ your mind, and they nev - er give ___ you
move ___ a - head; but the boss won't seem ___ to

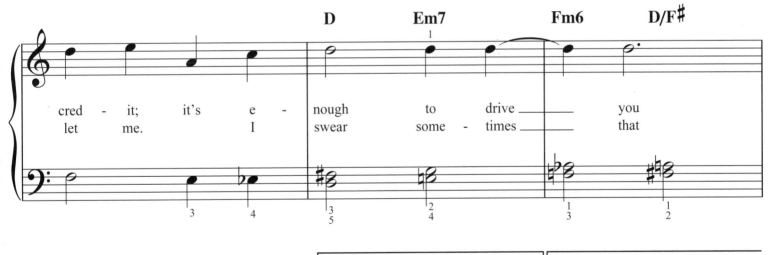

D   **Em7**   **Fm6**   **D/F#**

cred - it; it's e - nough to drive ___ you
let me.   I swear some - times ___ that

G   **Am7**   **1. A#dim7**   **G/B**   **2. A#dim7**   **G/B**

cra - zy if ___ you   let it.
man is out ___ to   get me.

D.S. al Coda

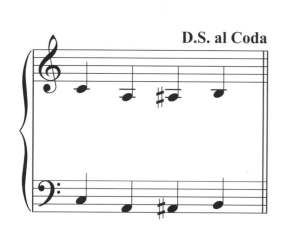

CODA

F7

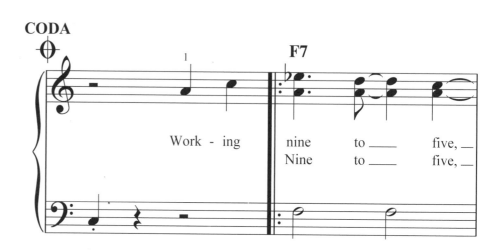

Work - ing nine to _____ five, _____
Nine to _____ five, _____

_____ what a way to make _____ a liv - ing; bare - ly
_____ they've got you where _____ they want _____ you; there's a

C

get - ting by, it's all tak - ing and _____ no
bet - ter life, and all you dream a - bout _____ it,

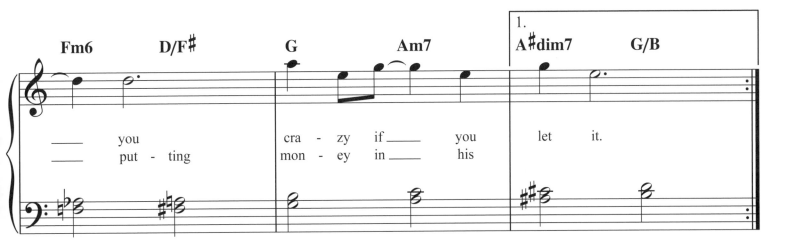

NOTHING'S GONNA STOP US NOW

from MANNEQUIN

Words and Music by DIANE WARREN
and ALBERT HAMMOND

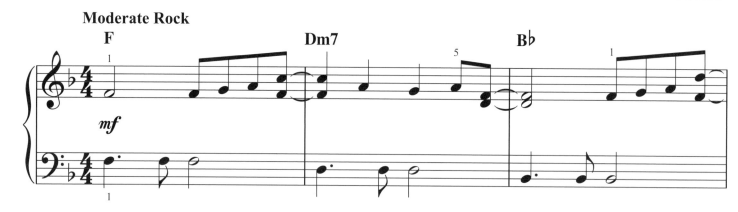

Look - ing in your eyes I see ___ a par - a - dise, this world ___
___ so glad I found you, I'm ___ not gon - na lose you, what - ev -

___ that I found ___ is too good ___ to be true. ___ Stand - ing here be - side you, want ___
- er it takes ___ I will stay ___ here with you. ___ Take ___ you to the good times, see ___

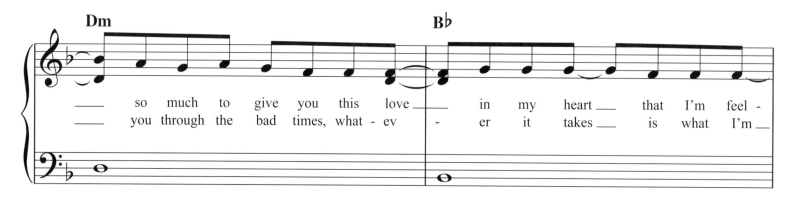

___ so much to give you this love ___ in my heart ___ that I'm feel -
you through the bad times, what - ev - er it takes ___ is what I'm ___

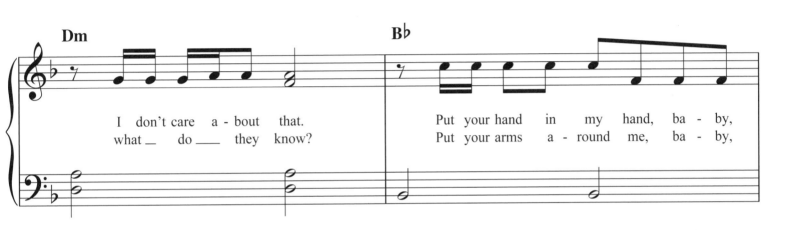

And we can build ___ this dream to - geth - er, stand - ing strong for - ev - er, noth -

- ing's gon - na stop us now. ___ And if this world ___ runs out of lov - ers, we'll ___

___ still have each oth - er, noth - ing's gon - na stop us, noth -

1.
- ing's gon - na stop us. I'm ___

2.
- ing's gon - na stop us. Oh,

all that I need ___ is you, you're all I ev - er

need. _____ All that I want ___ to do _____ is

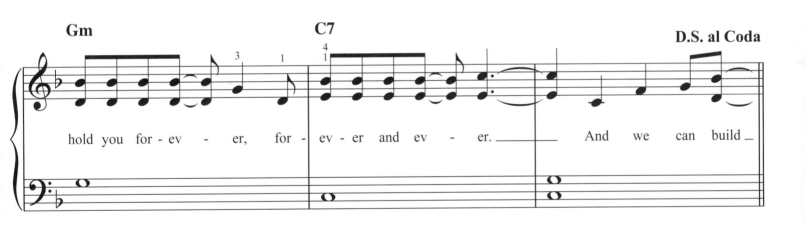

hold you for - ev - er, for - ev - er and ev - er. _____ And we can build ___

- ing's gon - na stop us.

THE POWER OF LOVE

featured in the Motion Picture BACK TO THE FUTURE

Words and Music by JOHNNY COLLA,
CHRIS HAYES and HUEY LEWIS

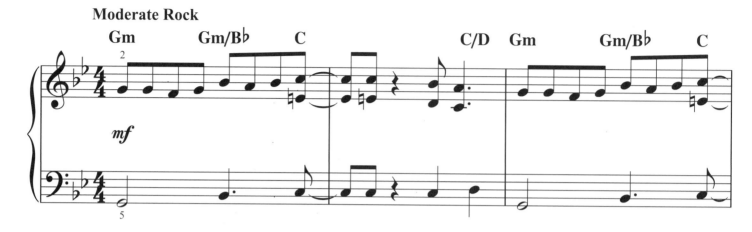

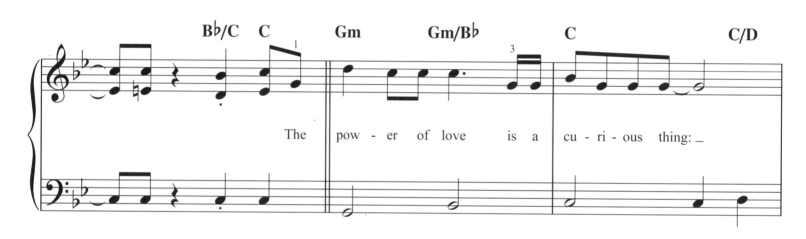

The pow-er of love is a cu-ri-ous thing:

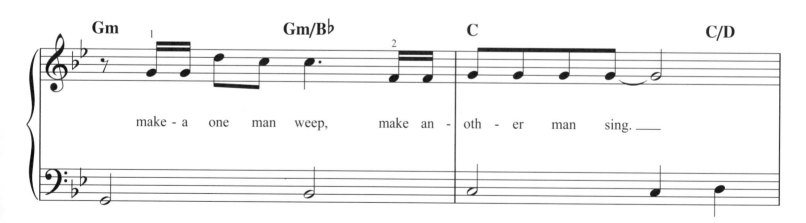

make-a one man weep, make an-oth-er man sing.

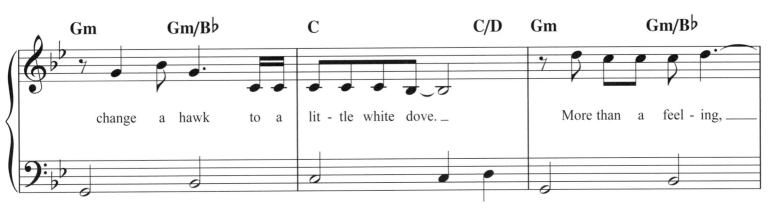

change a hawk to a lit - tle white dove. _ More than a feel - ing, _

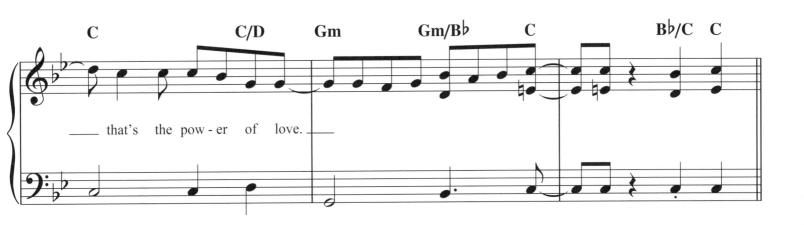

_ that's the pow - er of love. _

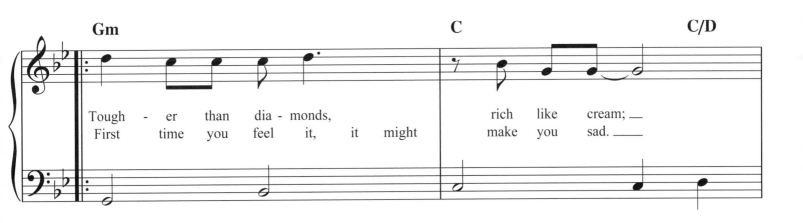

Tough - er than dia - monds, rich like cream; _
First time you feel it, it might make you sad. _

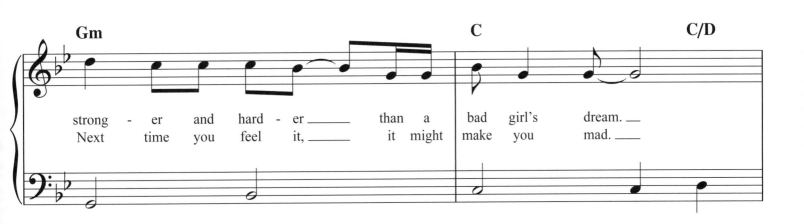

strong - er and hard - er _ than a bad girl's dream. _
Next time you feel it, _ it might make you mad. _

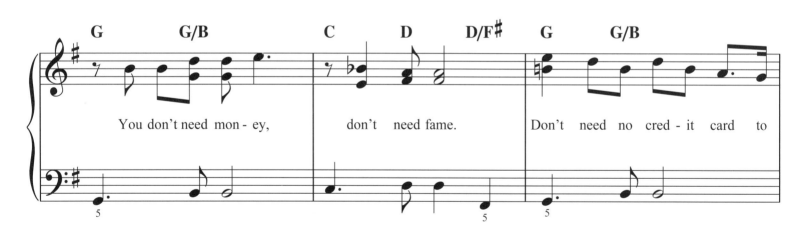

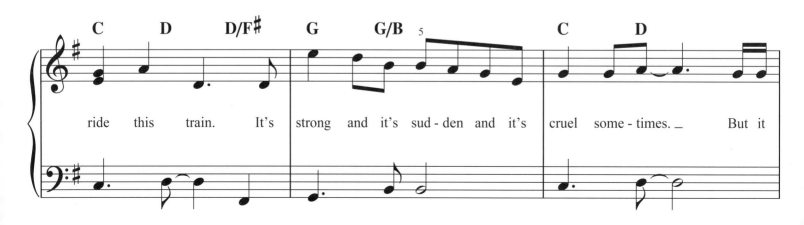

might just save __ your life.   That's the pow - er of

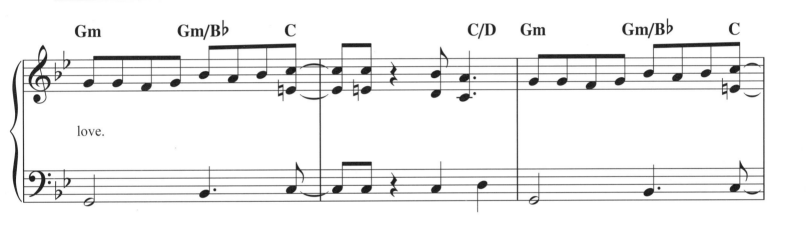

love.

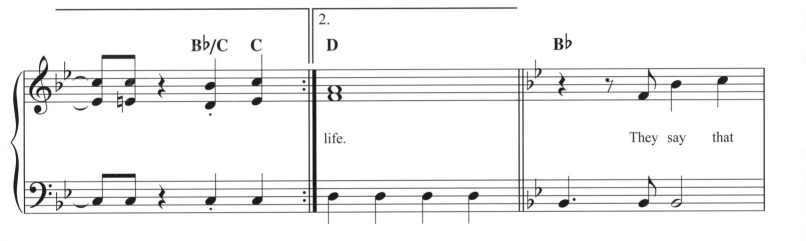

life.   They say that

all in love __ is   fair, _____ yeah, but   you don't care. _____

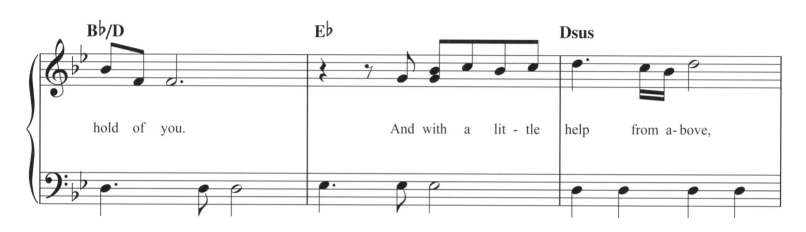

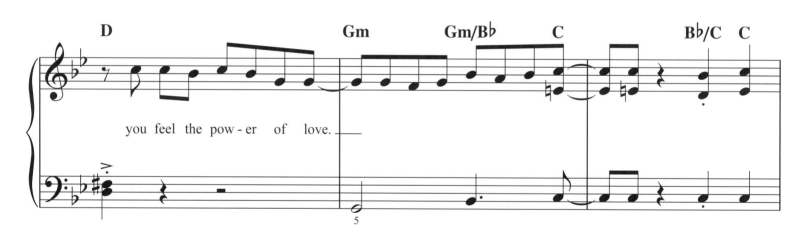

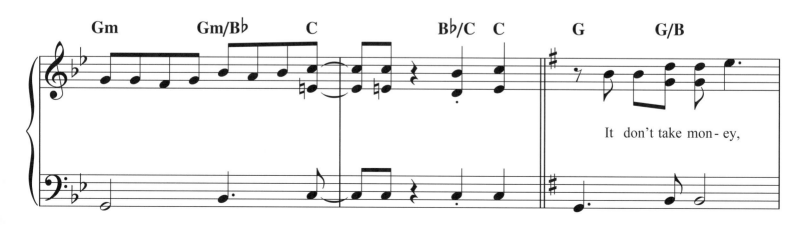

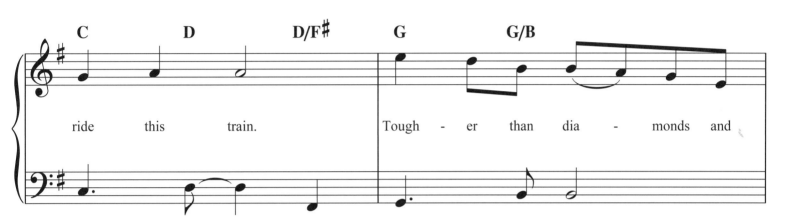

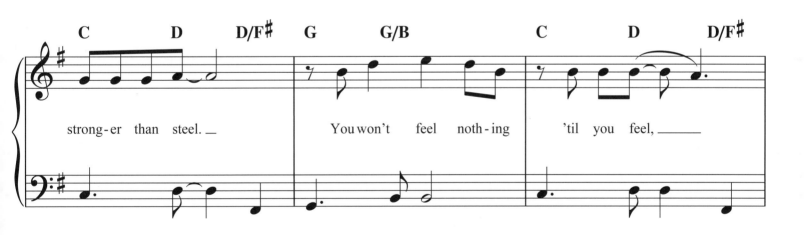

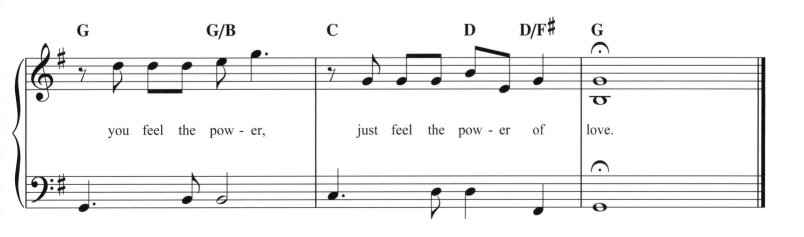

RAINDROPS KEEP FALLIN' ON MY HEAD

from BUTCH CASSIDY AND THE SUNDANCE KID

Lyric by HAL DAVID
Music by BURT BACHARACH

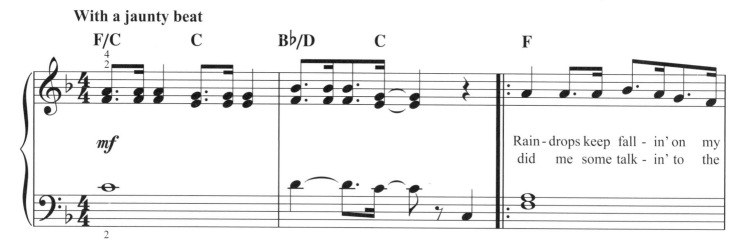

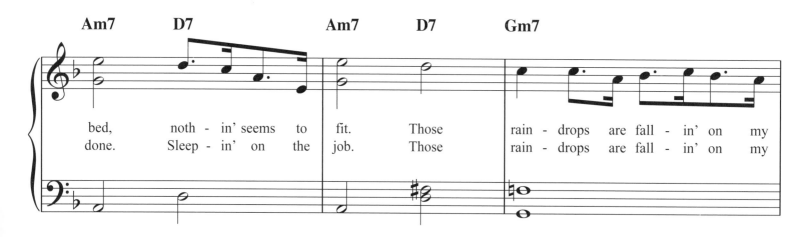

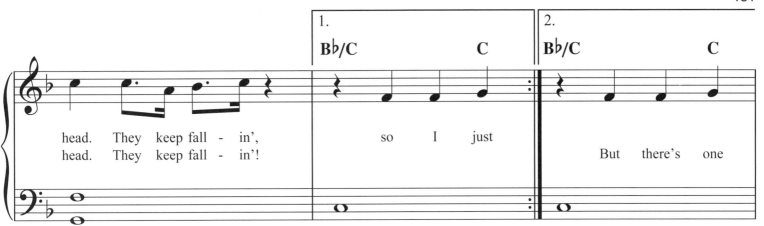

head.   They keep fall - in',

head.   They keep fall - in'!

so   I   just

But there's one

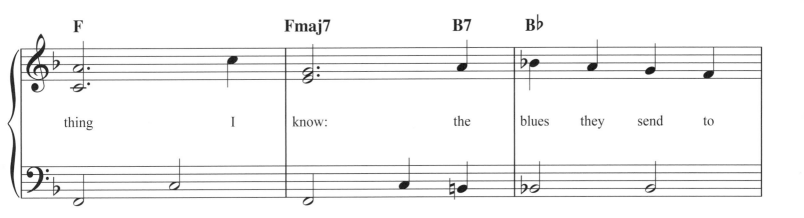

thing   I   know: the blues they send to

meet me won't de - feat me.   It won't be long till

hap - pi - ness steps up to greet ___ me.

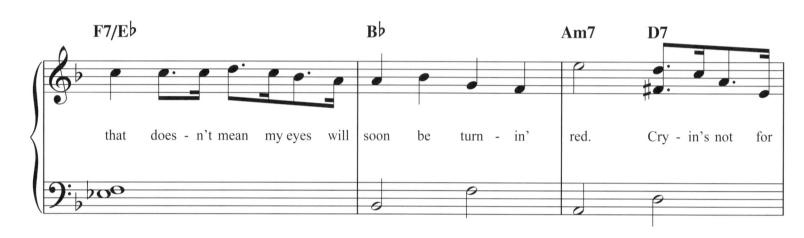

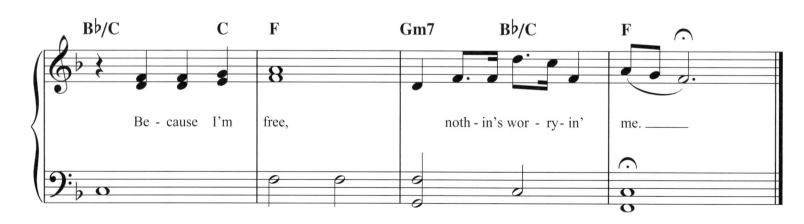

SAY YOU, SAY ME
from the Motion Picture WHITE NIGHTS

Words and Music by
LIONEL RICHIE

154

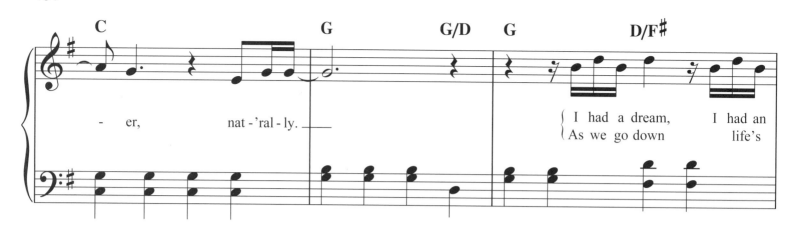

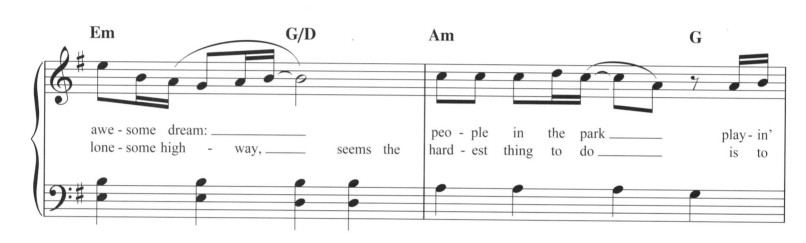

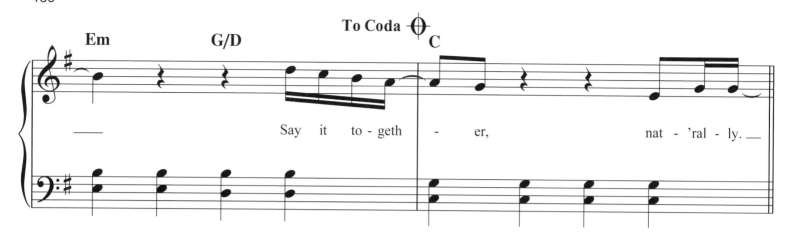

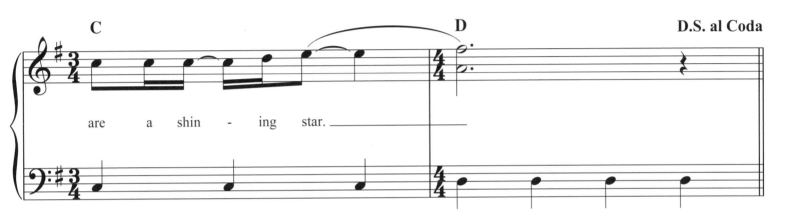

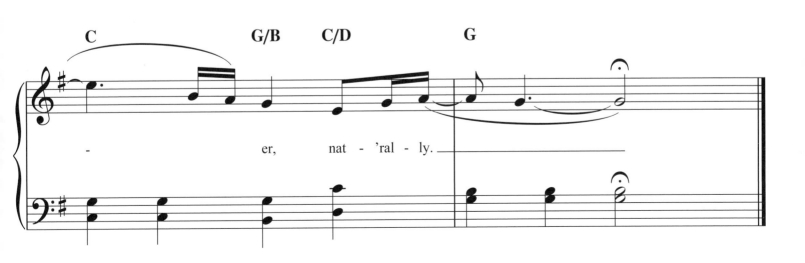

ST. ELMO'S FIRE
(Man in Motion)
from the Motion Picture ST. ELMO'S FIRE

Words by JOHN PARR
Music by DAVID FOSTER

Moderate Rock beat

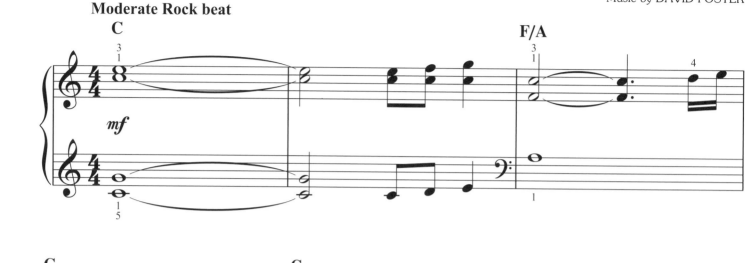

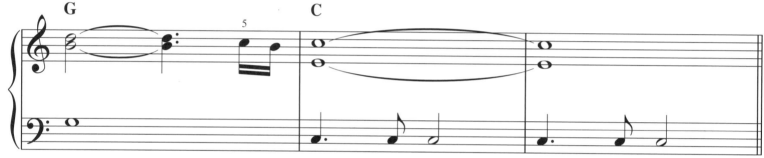

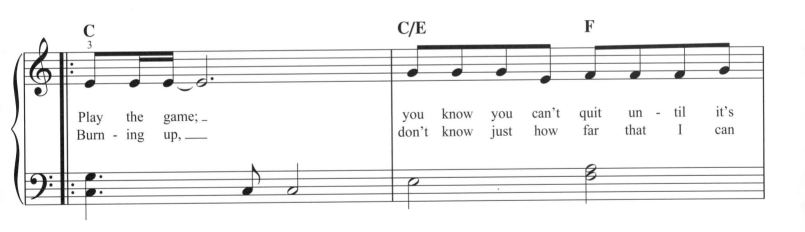

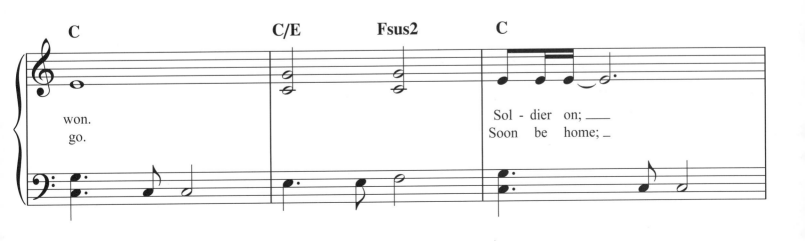

160

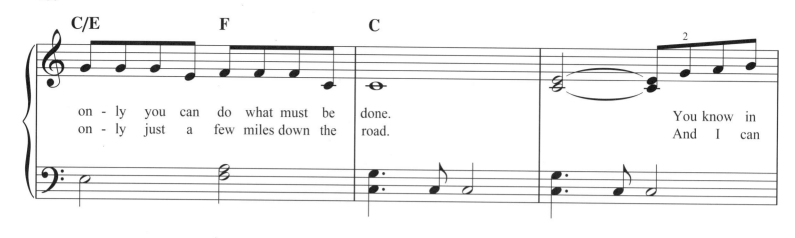

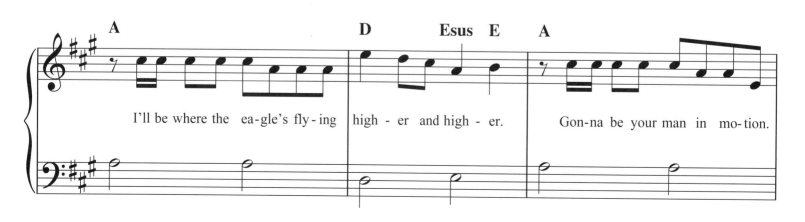

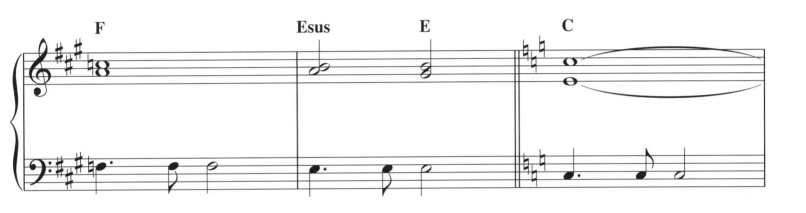

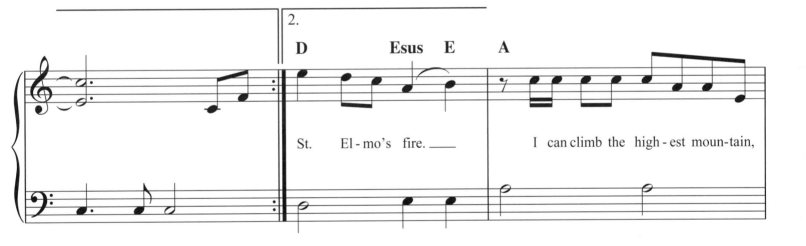

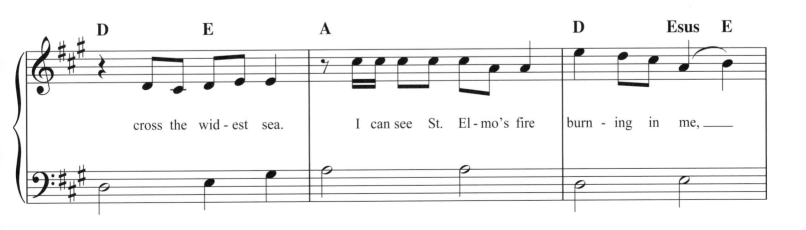

burn - ing in me. _____

Just once in my life a man has his

time. And my time is now;

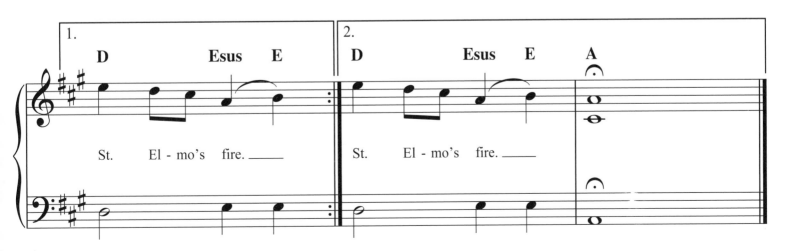

SEPARATE LIVES
Love Theme from WHITE NIGHTS

Words and Music by
STEPHEN BISHOP

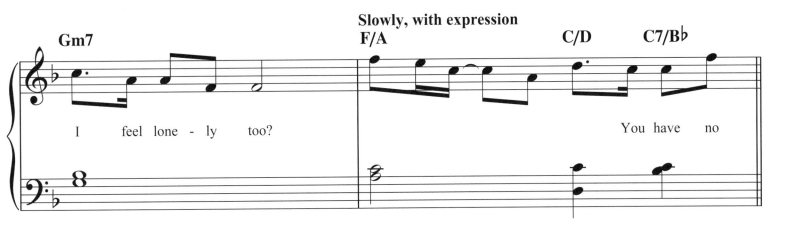

Slowly, with expression

I feel lone - ly too? You have no

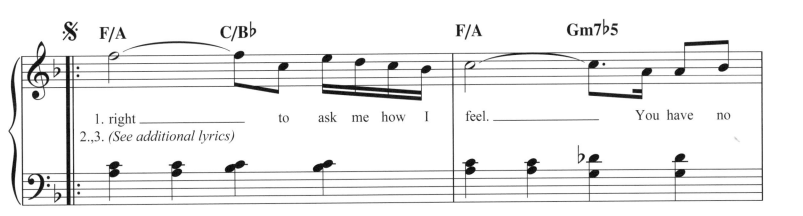

1. right _____ to ask me how I feel. _____ You have no
2., 3. *(See additional lyrics)*

To Coda

right _____ to speak to me so kind. _____ I can't go

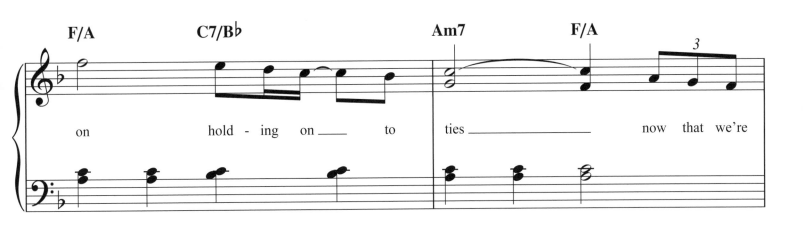

on hold - ing on _____ to ties _____ now that we're

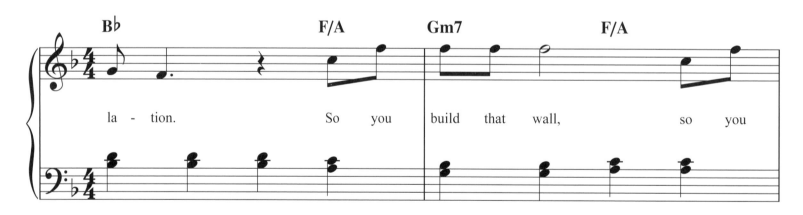

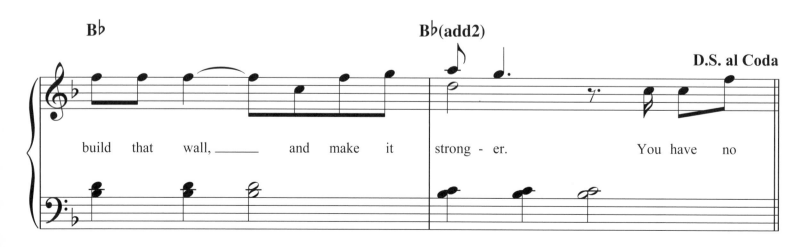

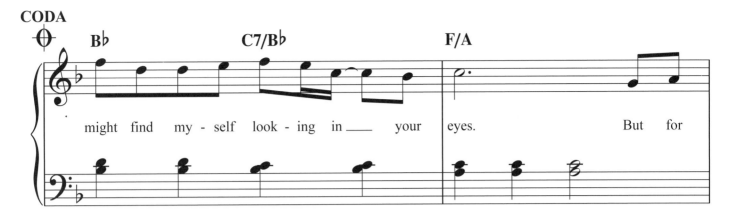

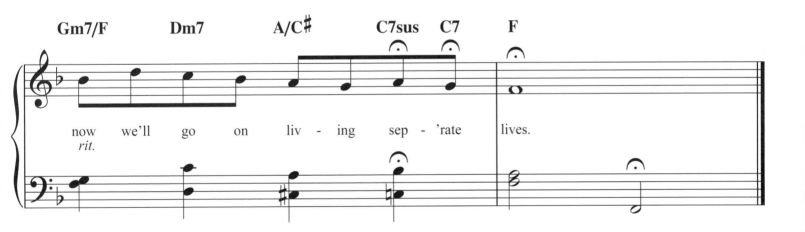

Additional Lyrics

2. Well, I held on to let you go.
   And if you lost your love for me,
   You never let it show.
   There was no way to compromise.
   So now we're living separate lives.

3. You have no right to ask me how I feel
   You have no right to speak to me so kind.
   Someday I might find myself looking in your eyes.
   But for now, we'll go on living separate lives.
   Yes, for now we'll go on living separate lives.

SINGIN' IN THE RAIN

from SINGIN' IN THE RAIN

Lyric by ARTHUR FREED
Music by NACIO HERB BROWN

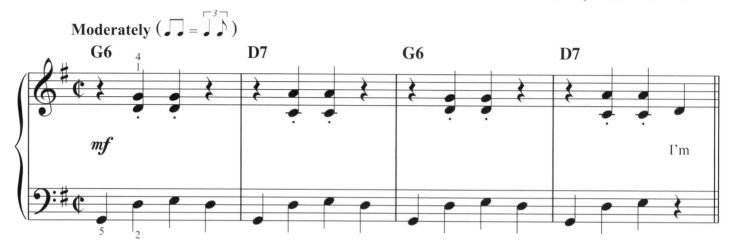

laugh - ing at clouds so dark up a - bove, the

G

sun's _____ in my heart _____ and I'm read - y for love. Let the

storm - y clouds chase ev -'ry - one _____ from the place. Come

G♯dim7   **D7**

on _____ with the rain, I've a smile _____ on my face. I'll

To Coda $\oplus$

walk down the lane with a hap - py re - frain, and

G6   **D7**

sing - in', _____ just sing - in' in _____ the rain.

E♭7   **G6**

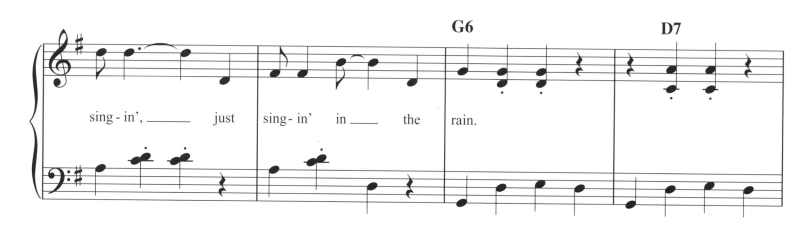

Why am I smil - in' and why do I sing? _____

E♭7   **G6**

Why does De - cem - ber seem sun - ny as Spring? _____

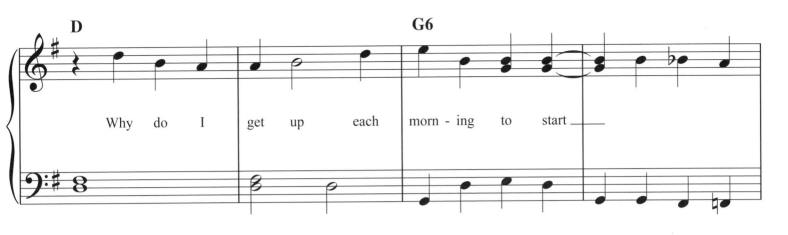

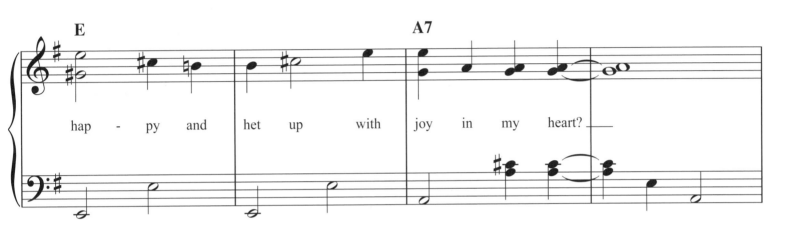

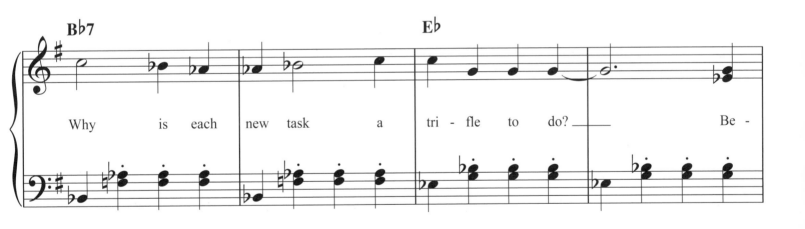

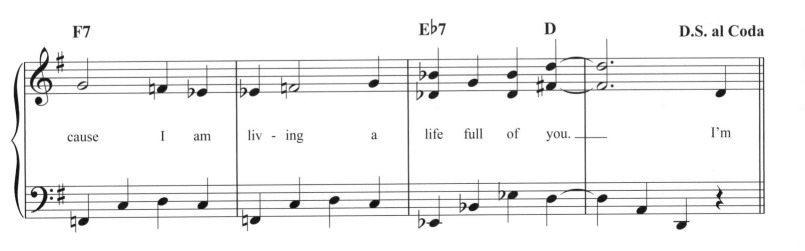

172

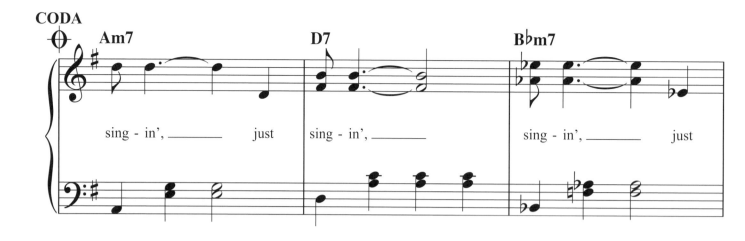

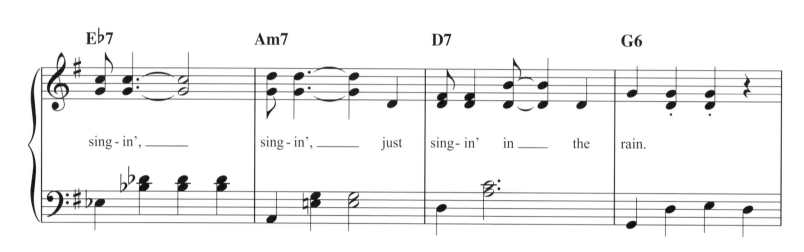

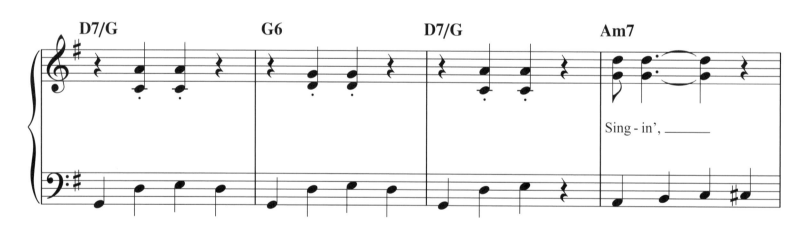

TO SIR, WITH LOVE

from TO SIR, WITH LOVE

Words by DON BLACK
Music by MARC LONDON

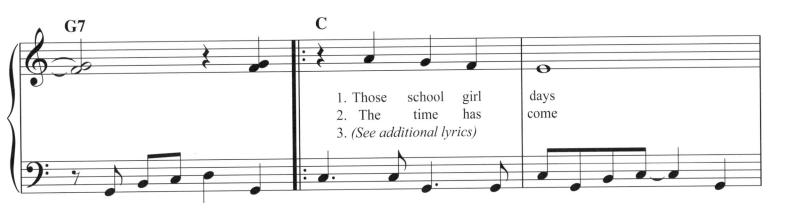

1. Those school girl days
2. The time has come
3. *(See additional lyrics)*

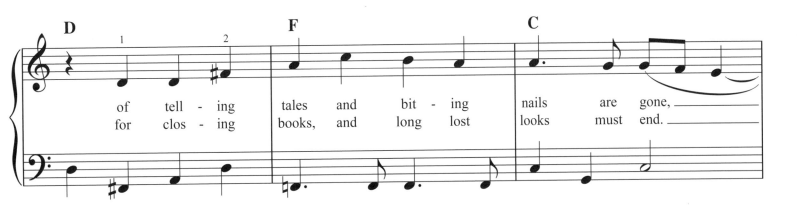

of tell - ing tales and bit - ing nails are gone, _____
for clos - ing books, and long lost looks must end. _____

_____ but in my mind
And as I leave,

I know they will _____ still live on and on. _____
I know that I am leav - ing my best friend, _____

_____ But how do you thank some - one _____ who has
_____ a friend who taught me right from wrong _ and

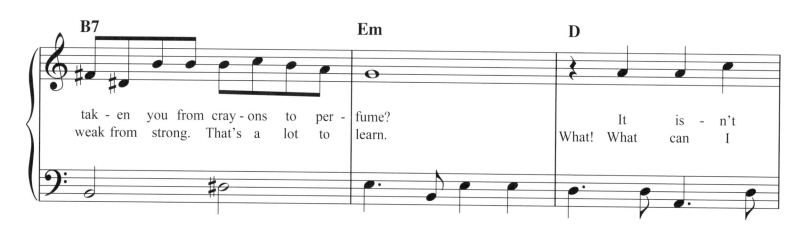

tak - en you from cray - ons to per - fume? It is - n't
weak from strong. That's a lot to learn. What! What can I

eas - y, but I'll try.
give you in re - turn? If you
If you

Additional Lyrics

3. Those awkward years have hurried by.
   Why did they fly away?
   Why is it, sir,
   Children grow up to be people one day?
   What takes the place of climbing trees and dirty knees
   In the world outside?
   What is there for you I can buy?
   If you wanted the world,
   I'd surround it with a wall.
   I'd scrawl these words with letters ten feet tall:
   "To sir, with love."

SKYFALL
from the Motion Picture SKYFALL

Words and Music by ADELE ADKINS
and PAUL EPWORTH

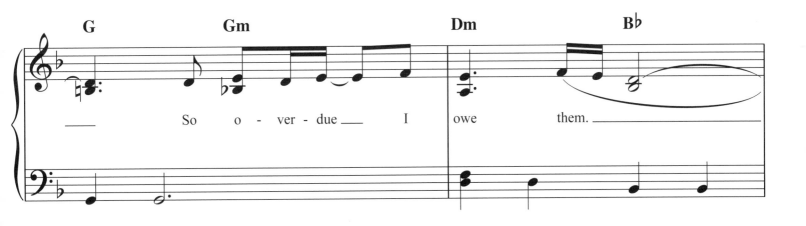

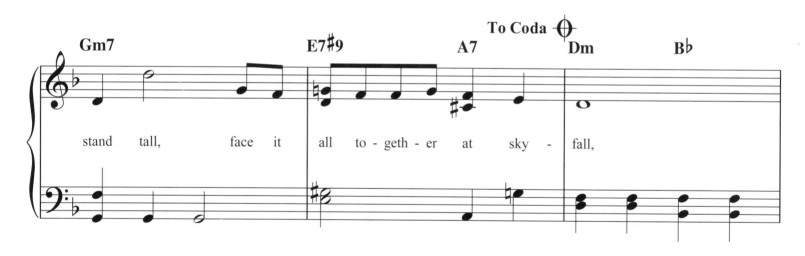

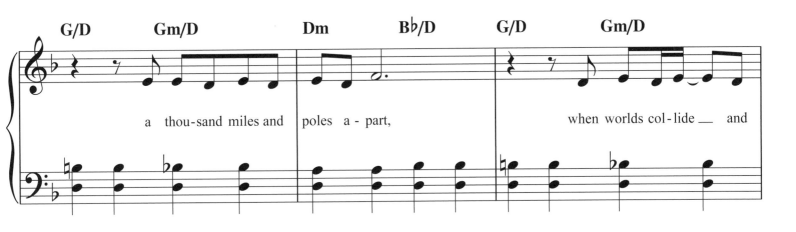

a thou-sand miles and poles a - part, when worlds col-lide ___ and

days are dark. You may have my num-ber, you can take my name, but you'll nev - er have my

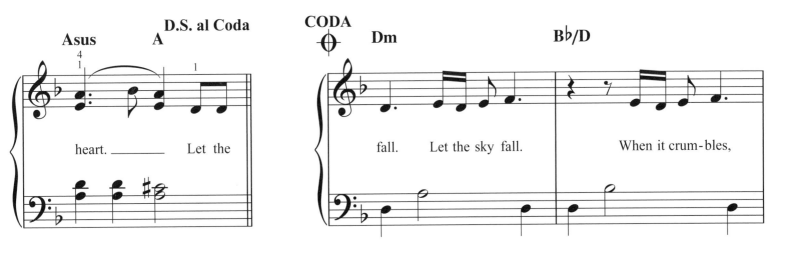

heart. _____ Let the fall. Let the sky fall. When it crum-bles,

we will stand tall. Let the sky fall. When it crum-bles,

we will stand tall.　Where you go,　I go.　What you see,

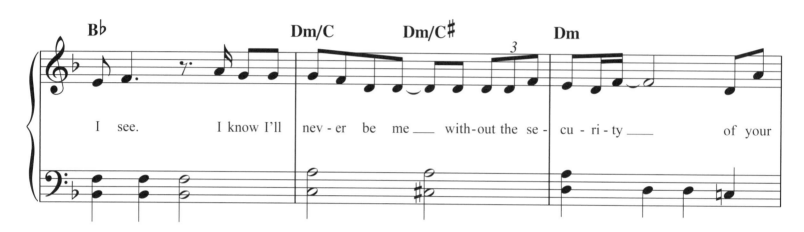

I see.　I know I'll nev - er be me ___ with-out the se - cu - ri - ty ___ of your

lov - ing arms　keep - ing　me from harm.　Put your　hand　in my hand　and we'll

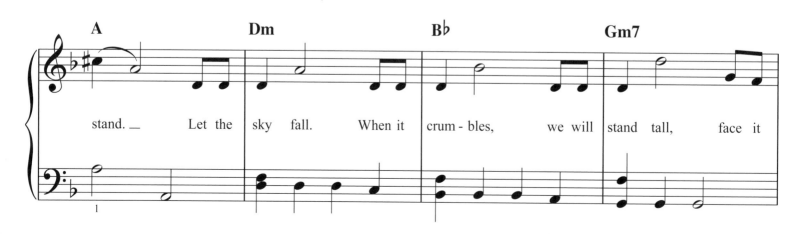

stand. ___ Let the　sky fall.　When it　crum - bles,　we will　stand tall,　face it

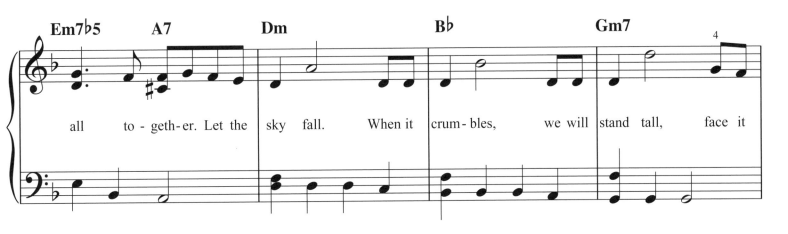

all to-geth-er. Let the sky fall. When it crum-bles, we will stand tall, face it

all to-geth-er at sky - fall. Let the sky fall.

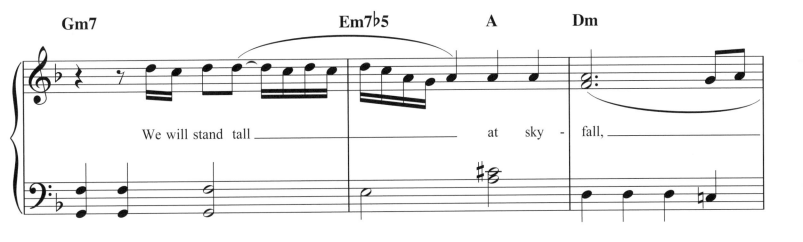

We will stand tall at sky - fall,

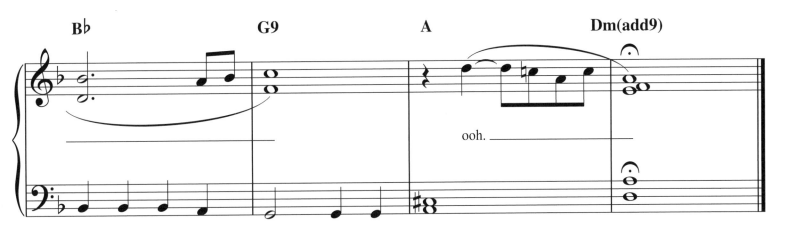

ooh.

SOMEWHERE
from WEST SIDE STORY

Lyrics by STEPHEN SONDHEIM
Music by LEONARD BERNSTEIN

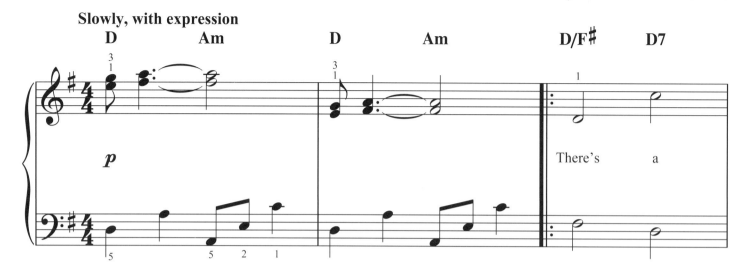

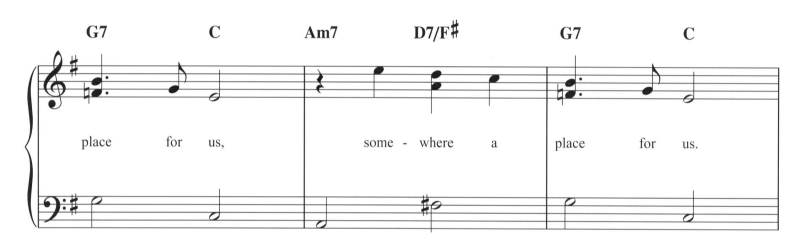

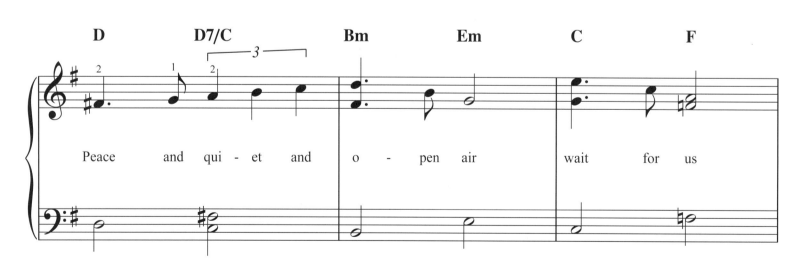

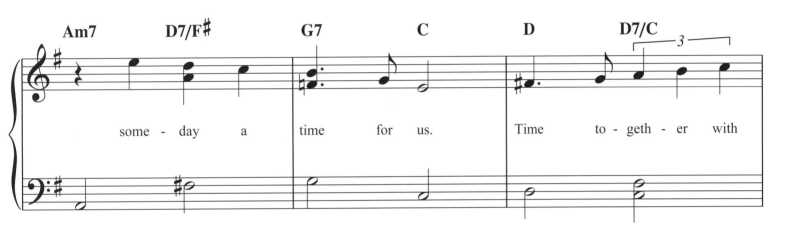

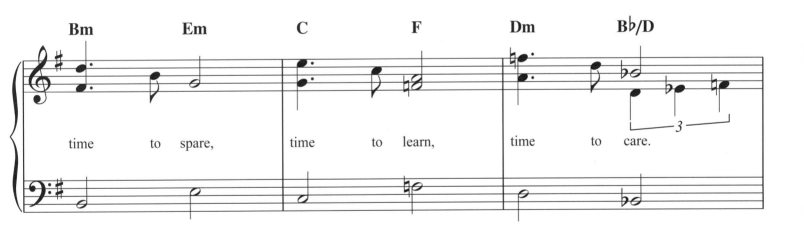

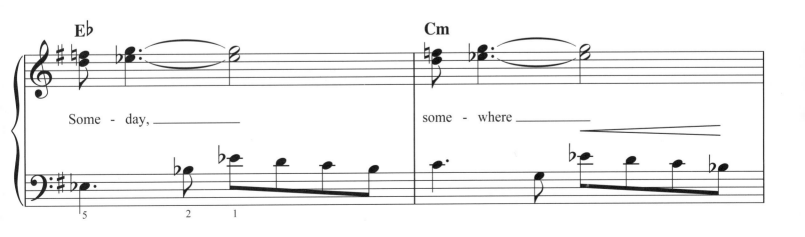

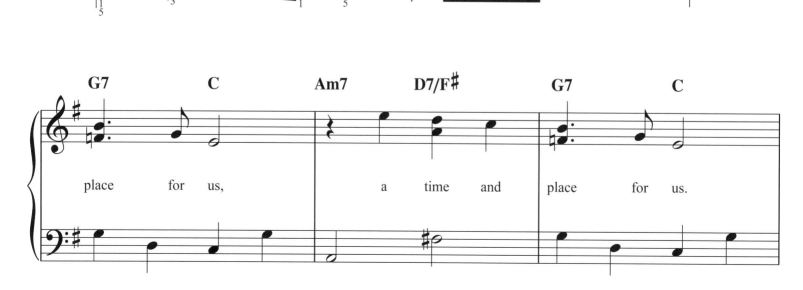

STAYIN' ALIVE
from the Motion Picture SATURDAY NIGHT FEVER

Words and Music by BARRY GIBB,
ROBIN GIBB and MAURICE GIBB

Medium Disco beat

Well, you can

tell by the way I use my walk, I'm a wom-an's man, no time to talk.
I get __ low and I get high, and if I can't get ei - ther I real - ly try. Got the

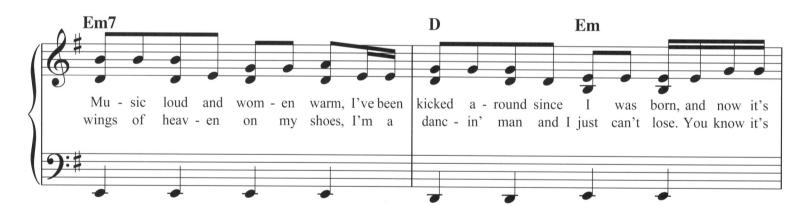

Mu - sic loud and wom - en warm, I've been kicked a - round since I was born, and now it's
wings of heav - en on my shoes, I'm a danc - in' man and I just can't lose. You know it's

all right, it's O. K. And you may look the oth - er way.
all right, it's O. K. I'll live to see an - oth - er day.

We can try to un - der - stand the New York Times' ef - fect on man.

Em7

Wheth-er you're a broth-er or wheth - er you're a moth-er you're stay - in' a - live, __ stay-in' a - live. __

Feel the cit - y break-in' and ev - 'ry-bod - y shak-in' and we're stay-in' a - live, __ stay-in' a - live. __

Ah, ha, ha, ha, stay - in' a - live, __ stay - in' a - live. __

Ah,   ha,   ha,   ha,   stay - in' a - live. ____

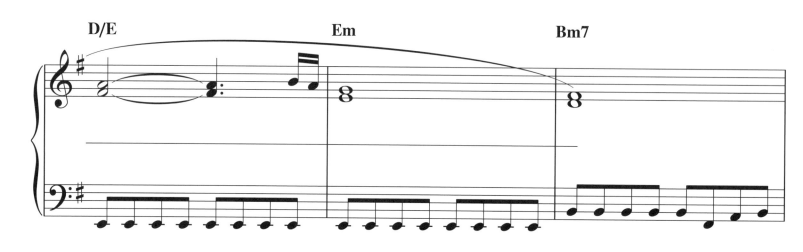

Well now,

Life go - in' no - where. ____

Some - bod - y help me. _____   Some - bod - y help _ me, yeah. _

Em   **A7**

Life go - in' no - where. _

Some - bod - y help _ me, yeah. _   Stay - in' a - live.

Em

(Theme from)
A SUMMER PLACE
from A SUMMER PLACE

Words by MACK DISCANT
Music by MAX STEINER

Slowly

Bells will be ring-ing and birds will be sing-ing if you and your lov-er should

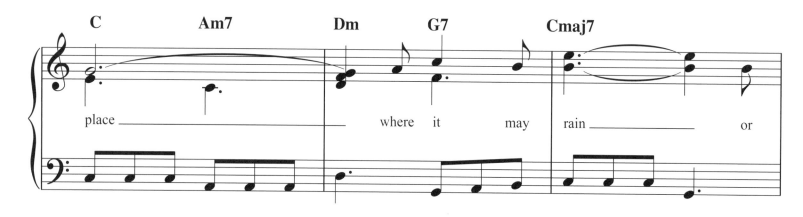

ev-er dis-cov-er that there's / There's a sum-mer

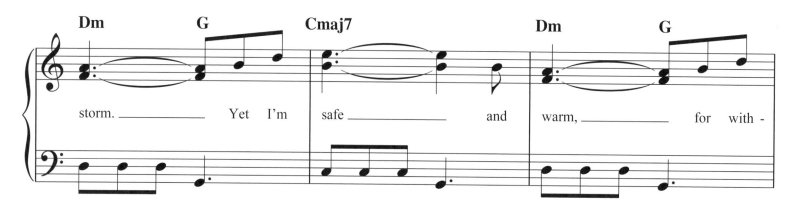

place where it may rain or

storm. Yet I'm safe and warm, for with-

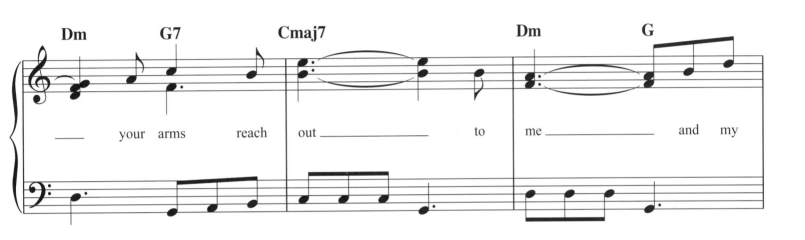

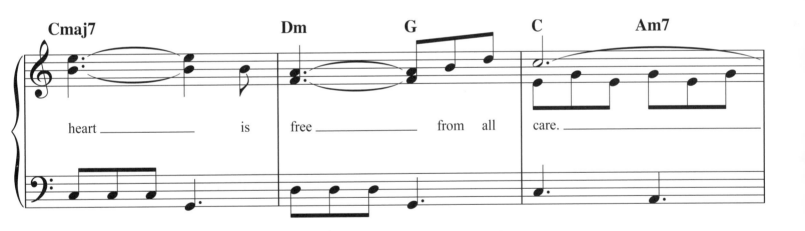

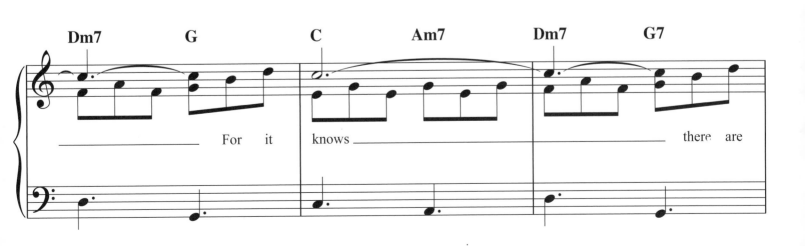

192

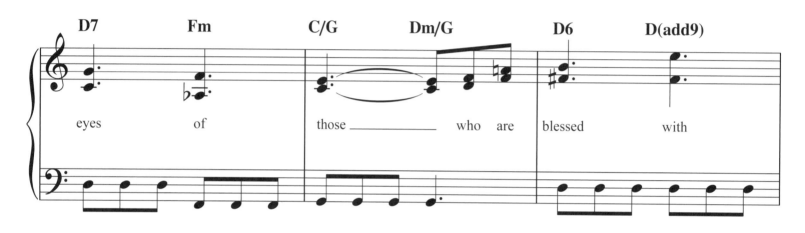

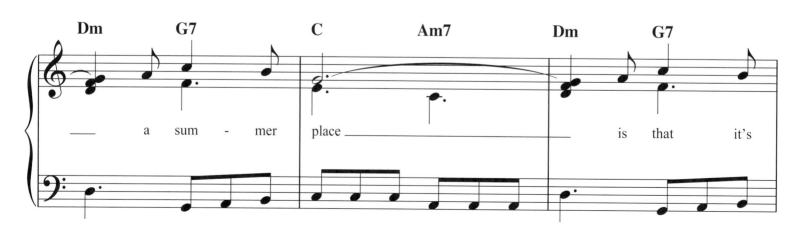

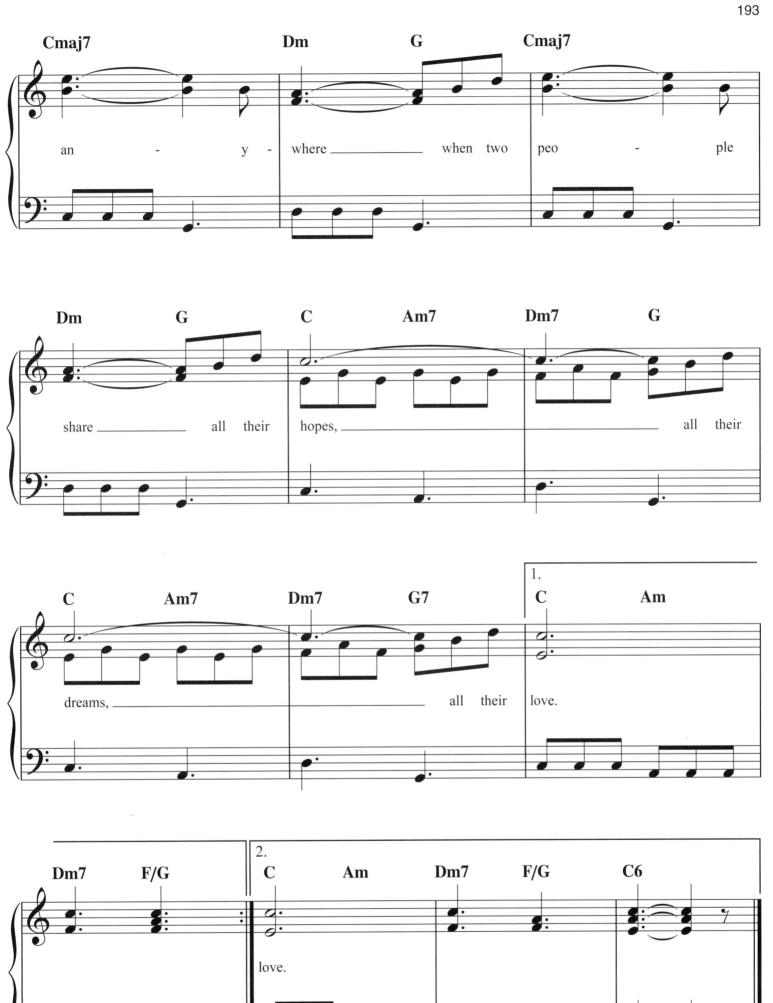

THAT'S AMORÉ
(That's Love)
from the Paramount Picture THE CADDY
featured in the Motion Picture MOONSTRUCK

Words by JACK BROOKS
Music by HARRY WARREN

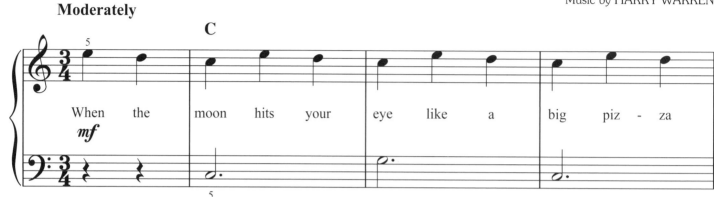

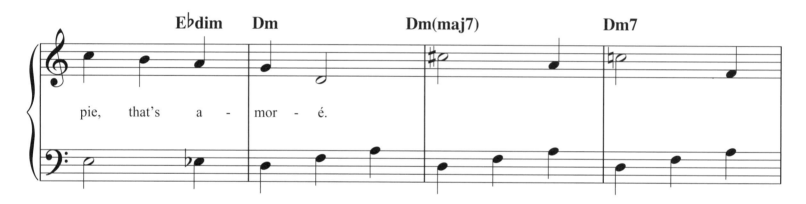

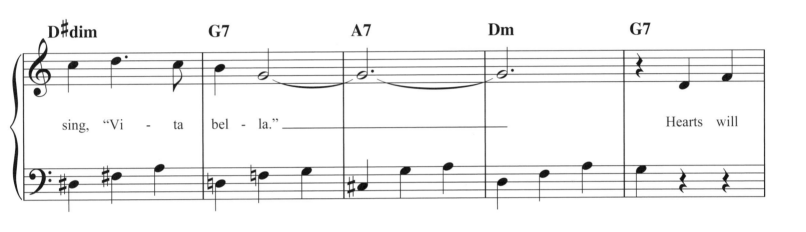

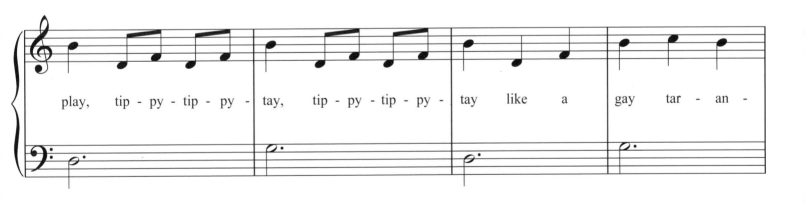

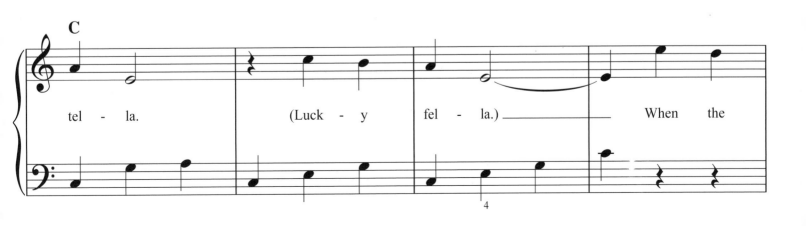

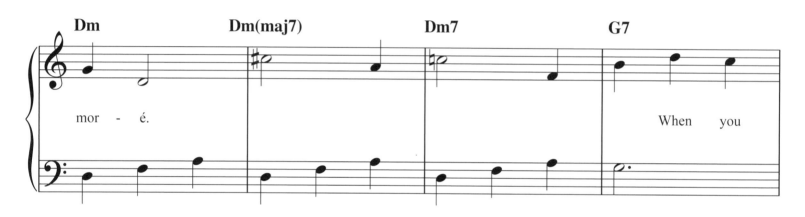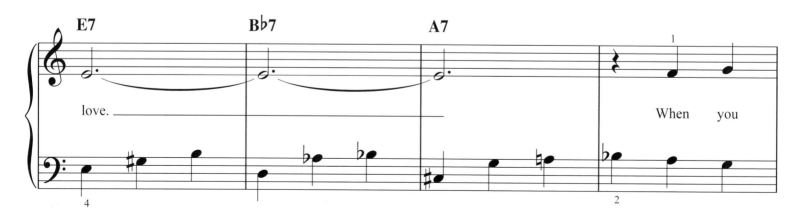

197

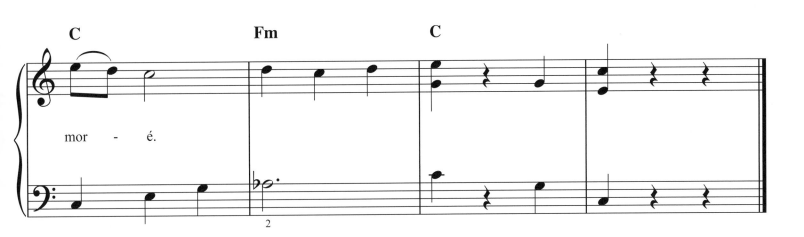

UNCHAINED MELODY

from the Motion Picture UNCHAINED
featured in the Motion Picture GHOST

Lyric by HY ZARET
Music by ALEX NORTH

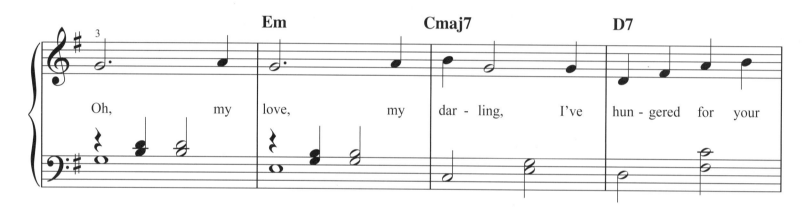

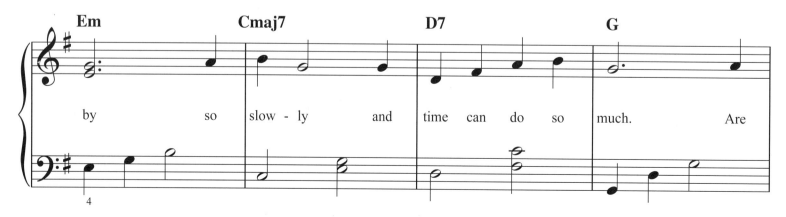

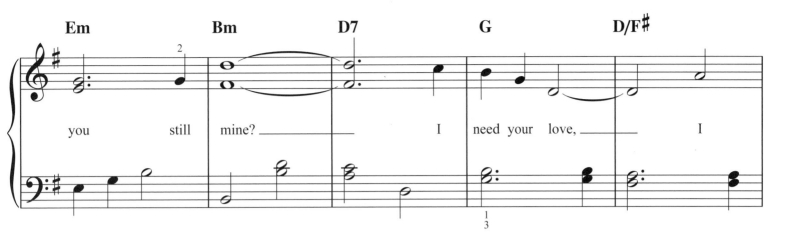

you still mine? _____ I need your love, _____ I

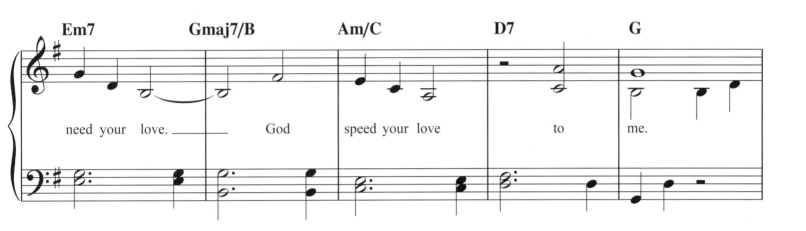

need your love. ___ God speed your love to me.

Slightly faster

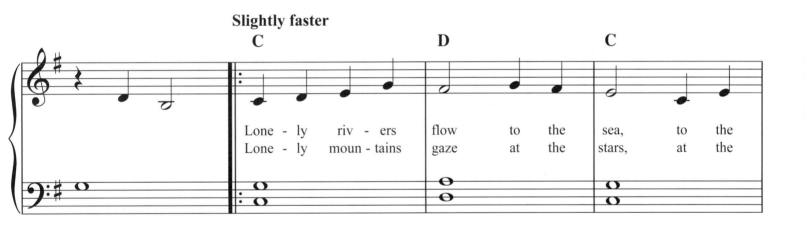

Lone - ly riv - ers flow to the sea, to the
Lone - ly moun - tains gaze at the stars, at the

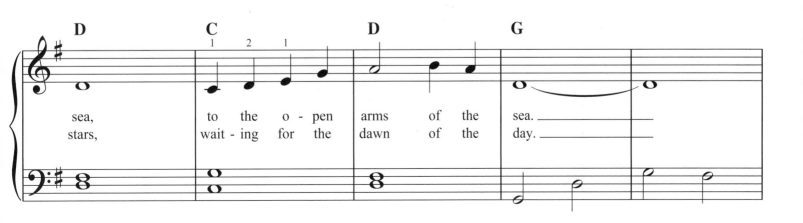

sea,
stars, to the o - pen arms of the sea. _____
wait - ing for the dawn of the day. _____

C   D   C   D   C

Lone - ly riv - ers sigh, "Wait for me, wait for me. I'll be com - ing
All a - lone, I gaze at the stars, at the stars, dream-ing of my

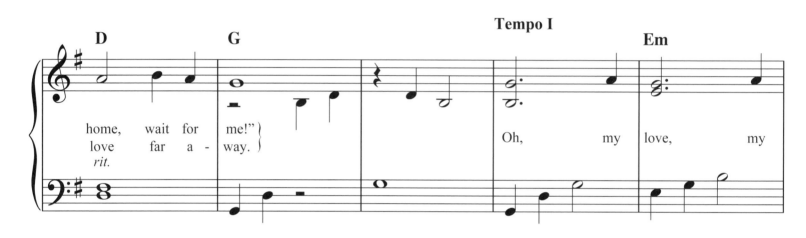

D   G   **Tempo I**   Em

home, wait for me!" Oh, my love, my
love far a - way.
rit.

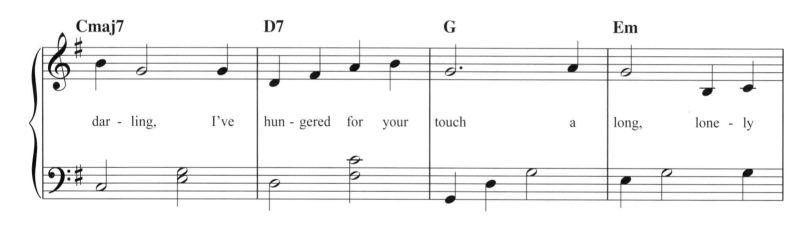

Cmaj7   D7   G   Em

dar - ling, I've hun - gered for your touch a long, lone - ly

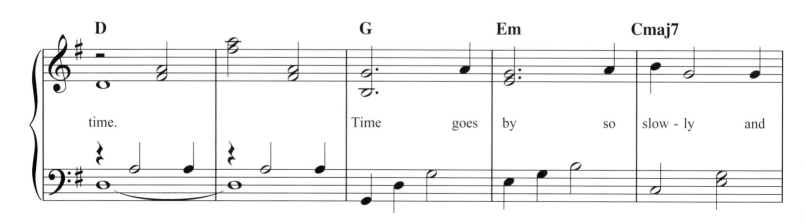

D   G   Em   Cmaj7

time. Time goes by so slow - ly and

time can do so much. Are you still mine? _____ I

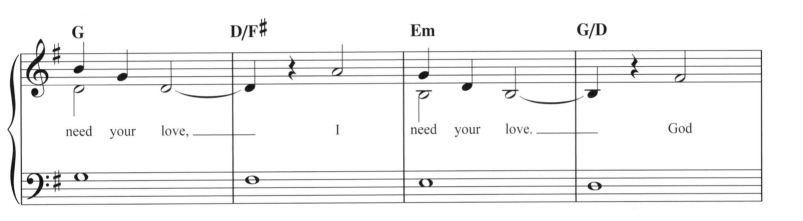

need your love, _____ I need your love. _____ God

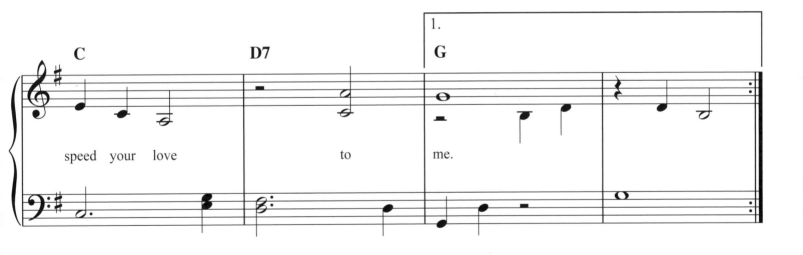

speed your love to me.

1.

2.

me. *dim. e rit.*

THE WAY WE WERE
from the Motion Picture THE WAY WE WERE

Words by ALAN and MARILYN BERGMAN
Music by MARVIN HAMLISCH

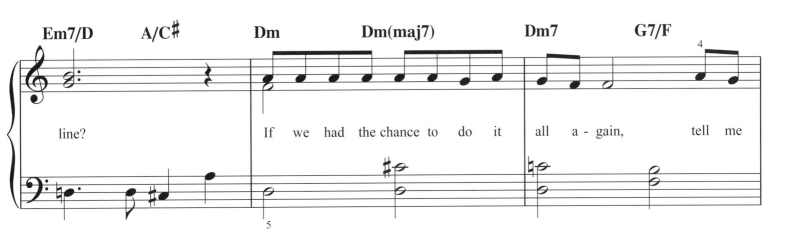

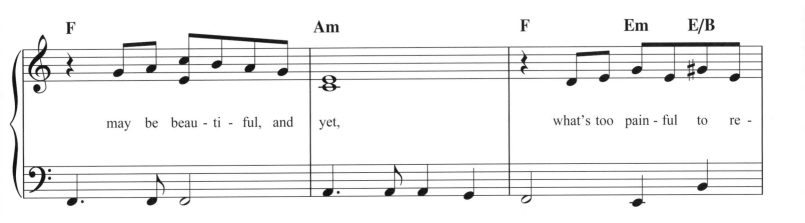

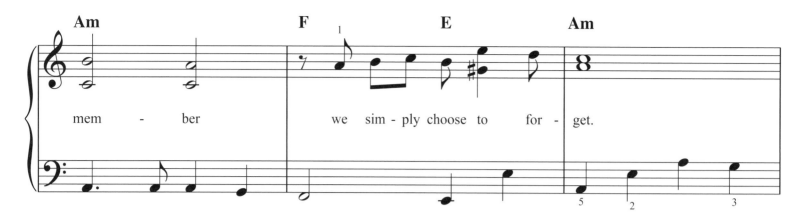

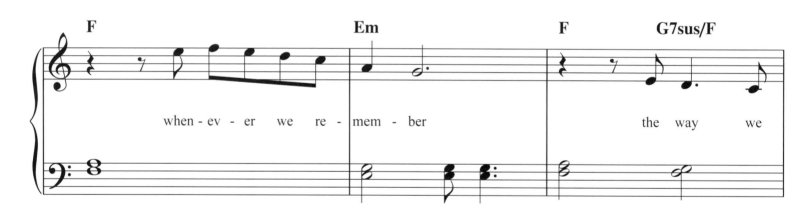

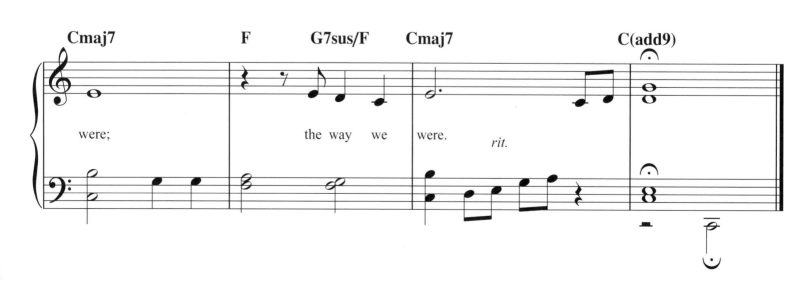

XANADU
from XANADU

Words and Music by
JEFF LYNNE

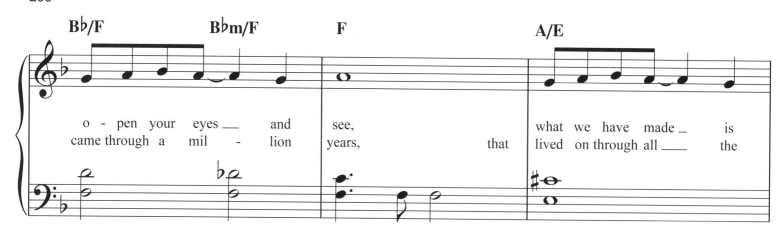

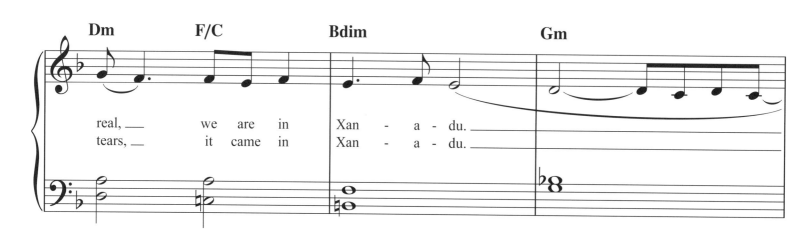

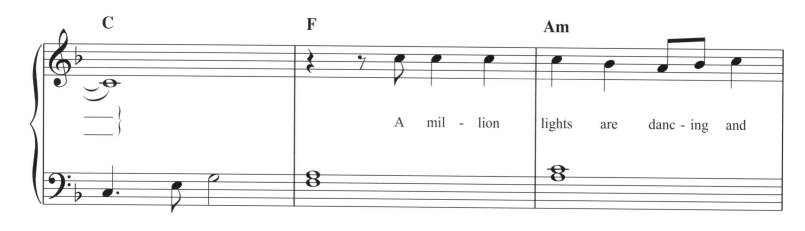

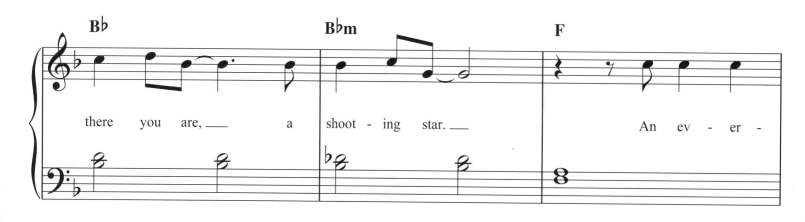

last - ing world and you're here with me ___ e - ter - nal - ly. ___

___ Xan - a - du, Xan - a - du, ___

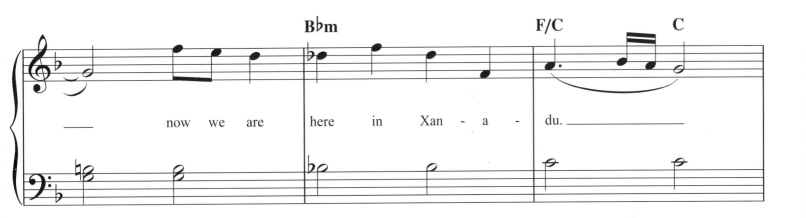

___ now we are here in Xan - a - du. ___

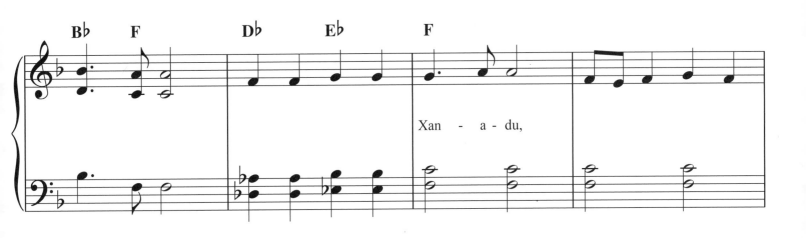

Xan - a - du,

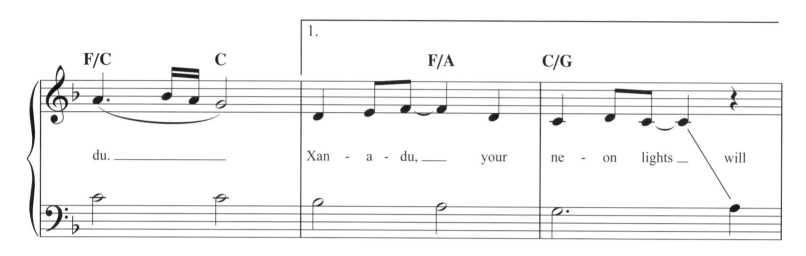

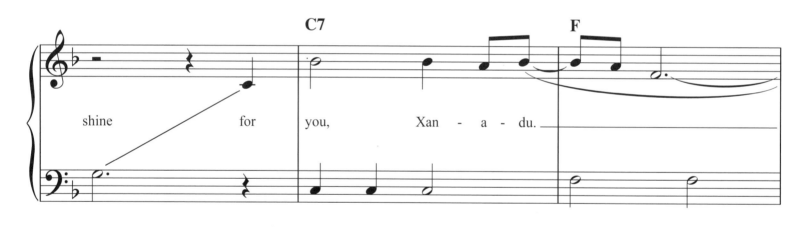

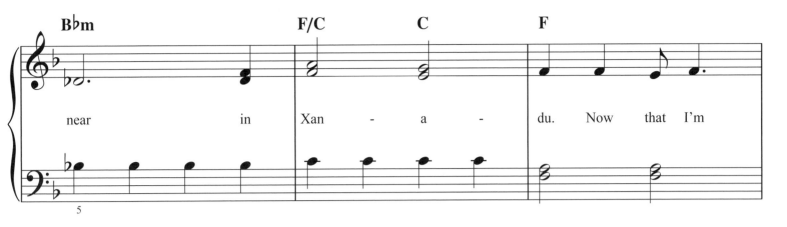

near   in   Xan - a - du.   Now   that   I'm

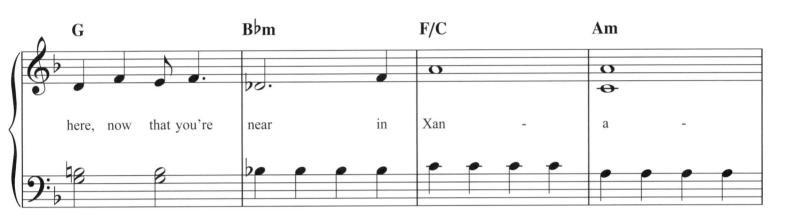

here,   now   that you're   near   in   Xan - a -

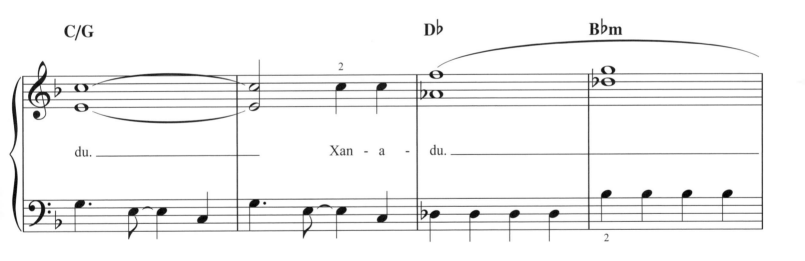

du. _____   Xan - a - du. _____

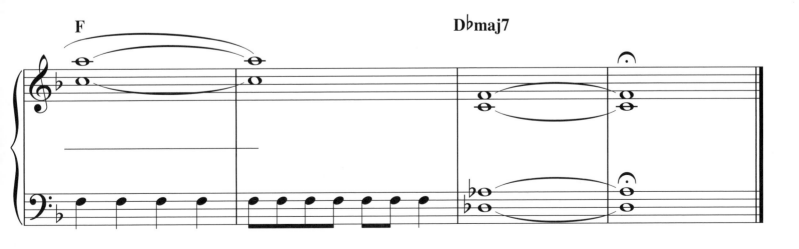

THE WIND BENEATH MY WINGS

from the Original Motion Picture BEACHES

Words and Music by LARRY HENLEY
and JEFF SILBAR

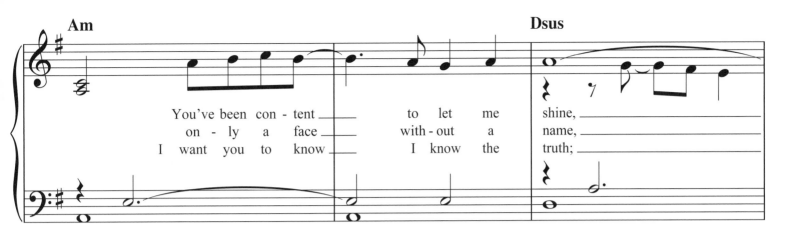

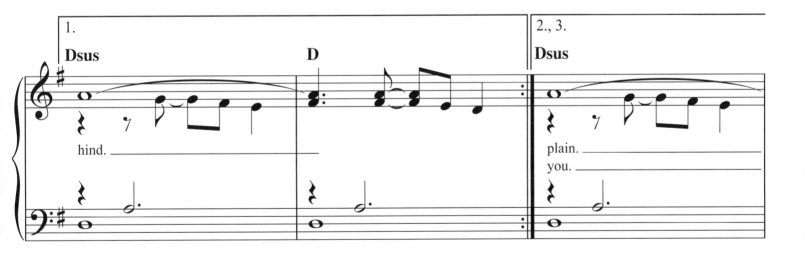

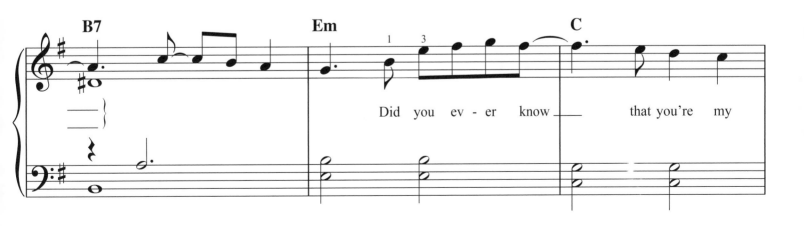

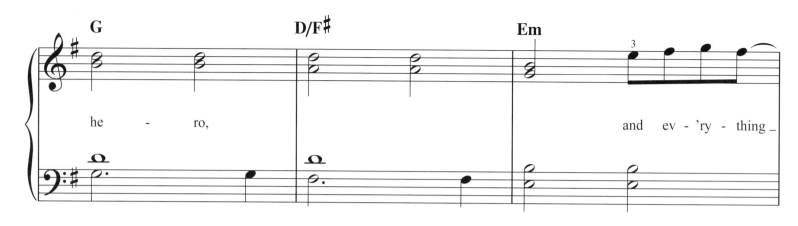

he - ro, and ev - 'ry - thing

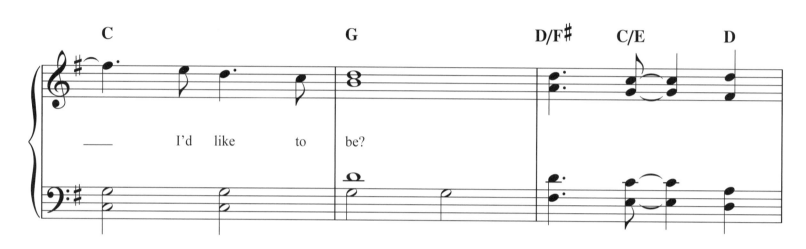

I'd like to be? I can fly high -

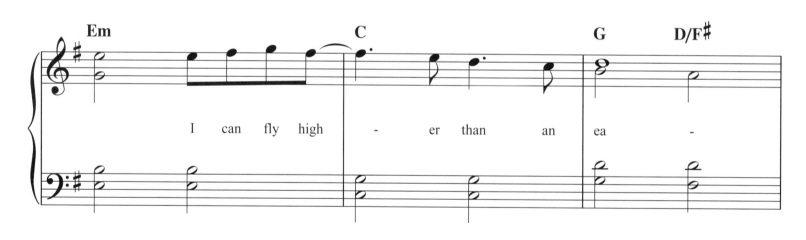

er than an ea -

gle, 'cause you are the wind be - neath my

wings.

D.S. al Coda

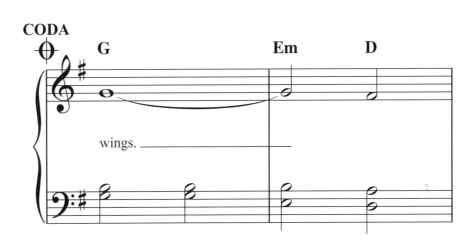

CODA

wings.

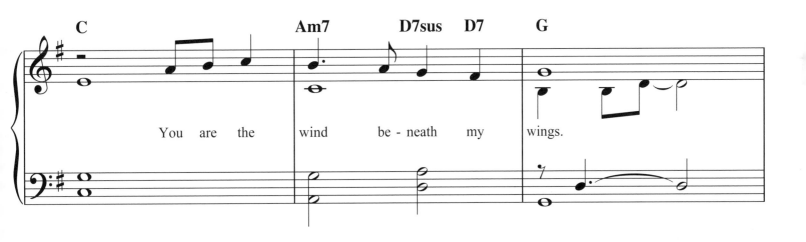

You are the wind be - neath my wings.

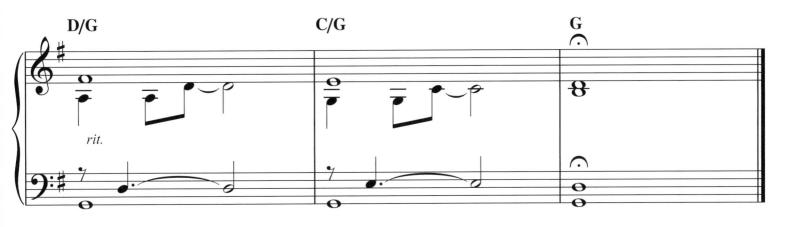

rit.

YOU LIGHT UP MY LIFE

from YOU LIGHT UP MY LIFE

Words and Music by
JOSEPH BROOKS

Moderately slow

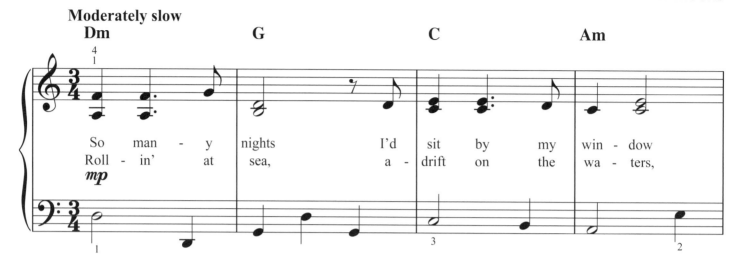

So man - y nights I'd sit by my win - dow
Roll - in' at sea, a - drift on the wa - ters,

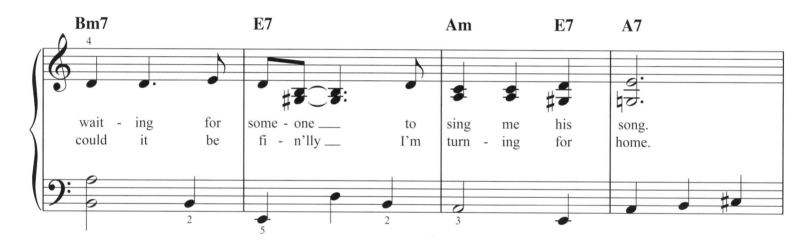

wait - ing for some - one ___ to sing me his song.
could it be fi - n'lly ___ I'm turn - ing his for home.

So man - y dreams I kept deep in - side me, a-
Fi - n'lly a chance to say, "Hey! I love you."

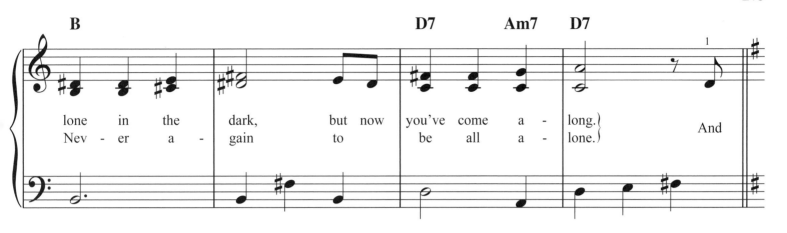

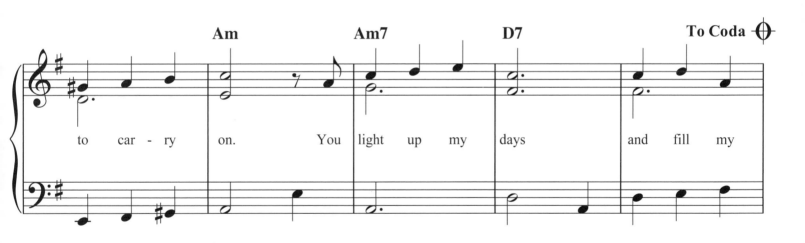

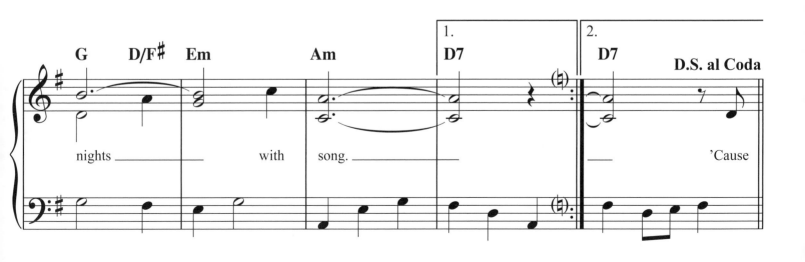

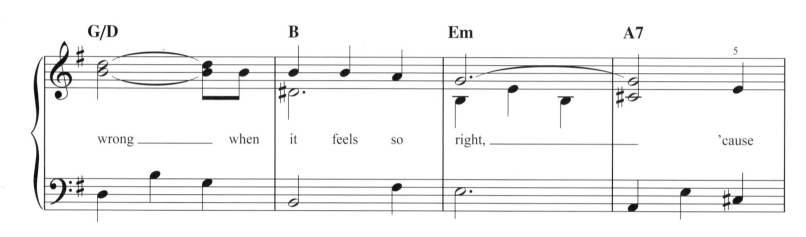

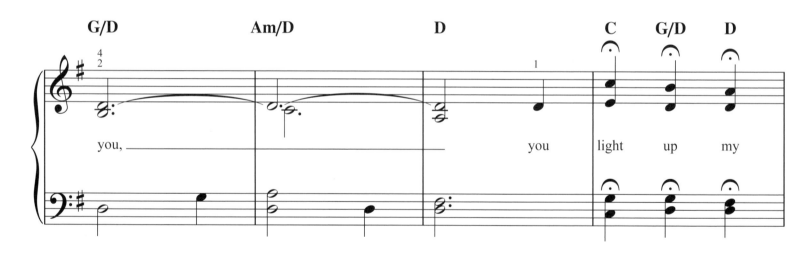

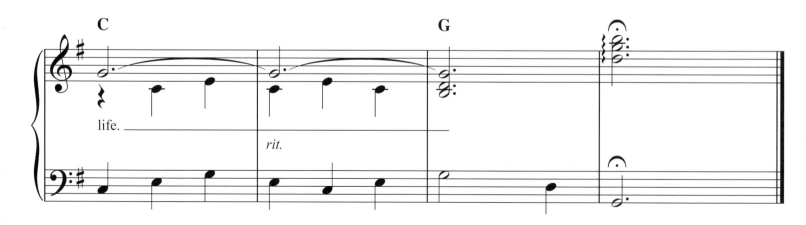